T0090287

Dog Sports

The Good, The Bad & The Stupid

A. Newman

*Our mission is to efficiently provide the world's finest, most comprehensive book publishing
service, enabling every author to experience success. To find out how to publish your book, your
way, and have it available worldwide, visit us online at www.trafford.com*

Trafford rev. 07/28/2010

 www.trafford.com

North America & international
toll-free: 1 888 232 4444 (USA & Canada)
phone: 250 383 6864 ♦ fax: 812 355 4082

INTRODUCTION

Wherever and whenever dog people gather, there are stories, some good, some bad and some just plain stupid. Hence, the title of this record of my experiences with dogs of all types, pure bred beauties, mix bred brilliant workers and everything in between over the past seventy years.

From the Bull Terriers that protected my family and I in the military quarters in India in the 1930's, on to the obedience champions at the British Kennel Club show, also the many average dogs that assist humans i.e. guide dogs for the blind, police service dogs as well as the many well loved, well behaved family dogs.

One of the first things that I did learn was never to judge a dog by the man made, and often changed standards of color and shape alone; these do not reflect the mental and physical ability to work for human masters at whatever tests and tasks the humans set and train for.

Structure, breeding and genetics have an important place in the dog fancy, BUT it is not the be all and end all.

I have tried to tell a story of my own life with the dogs and the humans who work so hard to train them.

Like all humans I do have opinions, some of which others will not agree. That's good is it not? Differences of opinions cause discussion, talking may bring about some changes, or not.

I do not apologize for my opinions, but please be kind enough to grant that I must have learnt something in the past seventy years and hope to go on learning in the years left to me.

Enjoy and disagree as you read, but first and foremost love your dog as he or she loves you.

CHAPTER ONE

IN THE BEGINNING

What happened to make me love and respect dogs, all dogs? I just do not know, it just happened and gave me a great life when other things were happening that were not so great.

My first memory of contact with dogs was as a small child about five years old, I think. My dad was in the British Army stationed in India, Mum had come out from England to marry, and I appeared a while later. We lived in a military cantonment; I remember being looked after by an Indian lady who was my Armagh, or nurse maid. Indian guards came on duty at night with huge Bull Terriers; they were not pets. They patrolled the area and were our security. My Mum caught me throwing food out of the window to the dogs, she was not happy about that and let me know her feelings in a very clear manner. Mum told me later that somehow I had got out of the house and she found me petting one of the dogs. It never bit me, just stood there with me. She recalled screaming at the guards, the dog and also me. Never again did I try to meet the dog.

In 1939 we were all shipped back to England as war with Germany was expected to break out at any time. At nine years old it was an exciting voyage. I had been attending an army school with army discipline; I can still remember the cane on the backside and the odd clip on the ear.

Back in England, a new way of life, new school and no nice nurse maid. It took time to get used to. However one thing I soon enjoyed was the fact that everyone in England had a pet dog as part of the family. It was a struggle, but finally Mum agreed to have our own dog. It was black and white and called "Chum". It followed me everywhere, even to the village school. My Mum had to tie "Chum" up in the mornings as the teachers did not appreciate an extra canine student. After school, running in the fields with "Chum", throwing a ball or chasing rabbits, but never catching one. I did the usual things as well; taught him to sit up and beg, roll over and play dead when I said "Bang". Life was really good until we all sat around a wireless and heard "Chamberlin" let us know we were now at war with Germany. The change was immediate, my Mum was appointed the head honcho of the Woman's Land Army Hostels, and we had to move to London. "Chum" disappeared, I was told he had gone to a farm to live, I hoped that was true.

Mum was busy, Dad was in France first, and then sent out to North Africa. Everything was chaos, food rationing, gas masks issued, black out at night, not a comfortable time. We were all waiting for the German bombers to come, and come they did.

Schools were so disorganized with children coming and going, some were closed, and some were destroyed in the raids. Some "trick cyclist" or psychiatrist as they like to be called had predicted that, without parental control many boys would get into mischief or trouble. I did. The BLITZ was on, not too bad at the beginning, but then every night and sometimes in the day.

I found a job as a Fire Messenger; it just meant riding a bike from fire station out to the firemen on the jobs. I became an expert at repairing flat tires, as there was a lot of glass around every where, I could also "jump" my bike over the fire hoses and other bits of junk in the way.

A big problem was the truant officers who tried to get the kids back to school, which was hopeless anyway due to school closures, etc. It was after a nasty day air raid that I made my next dog contact. Always, and I mean always, it was possible to get a cup of hot tea and something to eat from one of the Salvation Army mobile canteens, they were there when we needed them. Chewing a bun and enjoying a mug of tea during a break, I met a lady with a huge "Alsatian"; now of course better know as the "German Shepherd Dog". Hey, we were at war with Germany and people did not like anything German.

Her name was Mrs. Griffon; she trained dogs to search buildings and rubble for people trapped, injured or dead. She must have had a motherly instinct as she told me to stop smoking and clean myself up. She told me about the dogs, it was so interesting. I did see her a few other times, the last thing I saw was that she had been awarded the B.E.M. (British Empire Medal) for her work in the rescues. Everything was going quite well under the circumstances, and then the roof fell in. My Mum caught up with me. It was not a happy reunion.

She sent me up north to a farm in Yorkshire; she said it was for my own good to keep me safe. I had different plans but I lost the battle.

So there I was on a farm, not just a farm but one out on the Yorkshire moors, miles from even the nearest small village. From the excitement of London with a few shillings pay each week now on a desolate bleak farm. No shops, no cinema, no school and no pay.

I was not a happy camper; a laborer, cleaning up after cows, later even having to milk the stupid animals. What made it worse was that the farmer had been drafted into the army, leaving a very old man, the farmer's wife and a boy about my age to work the farm. I mean work, dawn to dusk every day of the week. There was just one good thing about the situation. It was in the food, the wife was a great cook, she made wonderful round bread loaves and pies by the dozen; meat, apple and cheese pies that melted in your mouth, lots of vegetables from the farm plus the bacon and ham from the pigs killed each year, or more often.

It became obvious, even to the old man, that there was no affinity between the bovine beasts and myself. One day he told me, the other boy would do the dairy work, I was going to learn the sheep work. I thought, my God, from huge brainless beasts to small and very smelly wooly beasts, what a deal.

That's where I met the two black and white BORDER Collies. After a while, with a few smacks across my head plus a few well aimed kicks to my butt, I began to work and understand the Border Collies. It became a dream, my life and attitude changed. It was wonderful to be out on the moors with the two dogs and hundreds of sheep, who were not as stupid as I had previously thought. Taking the flock out in early morning to graze, then back near the farm in the evening became a pleasure. Respecting the dogs, learning to drive, gather and cut out sheep from the flock was so rewarding.

I could not understand why the farmers treated their dogs so harshly, not allowed in the house, fed on maize meal and milk; maybe a rabbit or two if they were shot by the farmer. The attitude was that the dogs were tools, just like shovels, just pick them up when you needed them.

Without the two dogs the sheep could not be managed. The dogs did the work of ten men in a day; they were worth their weight in gold. The lambing season is the most important time of the year for the sheep farmer. This is the time when the farm makes some money or has a disastrous loss. It was decided that the old man and us two boys would go out on the moor to take care of the sheep. The old man was too infirm to walk very far, so we loaded him onto a farm cart with our supplies and left the farmer's wife with a helper to take care of the home farm work. Our home for the next few weeks would be an old tin shed on a farm cart. It held a water tank that had to be filled, a smoky old wood stove to cook on, the bunk beds and not much else. Light was by oil lanterns. Not exactly a home sweet home.

At the lambing site we unloaded the supplies and the old man, the helper took the cart back to the farm, he would be back at times with supplies. Now we were on our own. Now you will learn to work, the old man told us. We soon found out that he was not kidding. Before the sheep could be brought in, we had to build the folds. This was the fencing system. First dig holes with a huge crowbar to put in the posts, then drag, lift or carry large panel of woven fence and fix them to the posts. Hundreds of them, it took three days of long hours and hard work before the old man was satisfied enough to say that will do it. Splinters in the hands, back ache and exhaustion. Then I was told "go get them", be gentle and slow as many are pregnant and we do not want to lose any lambs.

Off we went the dogs happy to be working, slowly and carefully we drove the flock to the folds. The dogs were good and did not get excited as we worked our way across the moor. Into the fold, the old man checked each and every sheep. They were given some meal pellets and water. Then we settled down for the night. Next day a few lambs appear, the old man told us, not much sleep tonight boys, many are nearly ready to drop the lambs. As the lambing began so did our night patrols; wandering round the folds looking for sheep with problems. When we found them we had to help them, usually by pulling the lambs gently clear and making sure that they fed straight away. Sometimes it was not so simple and we had to call the old man. He knew what he was doing. For example, if a sheep died in birthing and the lamb was okay, he would find a "foster sheep", this also was not easy. One method he used was to put the orphan by the sheep, if she refused to take it, he would get one of the dogs to sniff the orphan, then the sheep would rush in to protect it and accept it as hers. Other ways he taught us were if the lamb dies at birth, he would skin it and put the skin around the orphan; the sheep would smell her dead lamb skin and take the orphan as hers. These are the skills of the sheep farmers, both to save lambs and put meat on your plate. I began to recognize the skills of the old man and appreciate the care he took of the sheep. I really began to respect the man as a shepherd, not just a crusty old man; the ways he could use the dogs and how the dogs seemed to know what they were doing.

To say I was learning to care for things other than myself was putting it mildly. However, things began to settle down and we spent a few more hours in the bunks sleeping. The shepherd began to tell us all sorts of stories about the "good old days", most of them he made up I think.

Very late one night we were all in the shed relaxed when the dogs began to bark and kick up a hell of noise. We rushed out and saw the dogs attacking a man, he was in quite a mess as the dog's teeth are sharp, and they were using them well to protect their sheep. A second man was trying to pull a sheep out of the fold. Both of us boys grabbed shovels and dealt with him very quickly. The shepherd told me to run to the nearest farm that had a telephone and call the police. I found the farm, woke up the farmer and he put the call through. I was on my way back to the folds when I saw a van on our property; the keys were still in so I took them and threw them as far as I could. Back at the folds they had the two men tied up with the dogs watching them very closely, I am sure that the dogs wanted the men to move, they had the sense not to try.

The County Police arrived and hauled the thieves away. I am sure they had to make a trip to a doctor as one was bitten badly; the other had a few bumps from our shovels. The police took statements from the three of us, they also said that the two men were known thieves and had records.

Later at their trial both men were sent to jail for five years for theft and black market activities, they were selling the meat to the hotels in the city. We were thanked, and that was that.

When we finally got back to our bunks, the shepherd really did surprise us. He said that we were not as stupid and useless as he thought we were, and then he shocked us by pouring a big shot of his rum into our tea mugs. It had been quite a night. After the lambing was over we all went back to the usual farm routines.

By this time I could work the dogs quite well with the sheep. I also began to get a little bit too clever. I had seen sheep dog trials and I began to try to work the tests.

First to send a dog out to gather a mob of sheep from over half a mile away, that went quite well. Next, I made a gate way with two of the sheep folds then tried to drive the flock through the gap. Not so easy. I think the sheep; the dogs and I became frustrated and fed up. I tried again with just two sheep, so far so good. Now to get six to do the same thing; more practice and a lot more patience required. Eventually I could manage it. Now for the big test, to drive six sheep into a very small pen; I kept working and even the dogs began to help me without being told.

Now for the first of my stupid tricks.

Each area organized a local sheep dog trial every year. I asked the shepherd if I could enter with the dogs. After he almost fell over laughing, he said why not, it should be a lot of fun.

So there I was on the trial field among all the local farmers and their sons, and believe me a great subject of hilarity for all. I will not dwell on the disasters that befell me. Either my whistle was "off key" or the dog was also joining in the fun. It was a complete disaster. Also, I did not know that I had to get the dog to cut out ONE sheep and bring it to me. I must have missed that part when I watched a trial down south. I did however take great pride in coming 39th out of the 40 dogs. My prize was a quart of beer, which the shepherd took, and a huge pork pie which the farmer's wife took, saying just right for Sunday tea.

Although I enjoyed the dogs and the freedom out on the moor, I still was a city boy. I knew that farm life was not for me. I began to miss the shops, the cinema and boys of my own age, getting up to tricks, chasing the girls and all that fun. The farmer's wife understood, she gave me some wages and bought me a rail ticket back to London. So I left the farm. Now what!! I knew what would happen when my Mum caught me. It did.

As the train rumbled towards London I remembered the last excitement on the farm. As I bit into the ham sandwich that the farmer's wife had prepared for my trip, I thought of the day of the "pig killing". Each farm was allowed to kill one pig a year for their own use; they had to give up meat coupons from the food ration book. Farmers are not angels. They saw the opportunity to get around the regulations.

A few farmers would meet and the plan was put into place. Any boys available were sent out to watch the roads for the food inspector's car. They would raise the alarm if any strangers came anywhere near the farm. Then the pig met his end, bled out, scrubbed and very quickly cut up into portions. Each farmer had a share and the excess somehow found its way to the big hotels or rich people. Yes it was black market, yes it was illegal, but farmers needed money so the rules were bent a little.

The train got nearer to London. What was I going to do now? Did I miss the dogs, yes it hurt like hell. Would I go back to the farm, definitely never.

I thought of the Bull Terriers in India. I remembered playing with "Chum", Mrs. Griffon's dog was on my mind. The Border Collies, what can I say, I would miss them so much. There was no way to get a job working with dogs as a living. Was I to become the forth generation of the family in the regular army? Was there any alternative?

The decision was made, it was the army. I knew the system; I would work hard and get promotions. I would also try to learn more about dogs and dog sports in my spare time. I knew there would be dogs some where in my life. So I forged my Mum's signature and joined the Royal Engineers.

Basic training over, I was sent to the assault regiment and a few years later joined the parachute brigade.

GETTING SERIOUS WITH DOGS

Think of the Parachute Brigade as a sort of fire brigade. When trouble broke out any where in the world, the Para's went out fast, doused the problem and went back to our base in Aldershot, England. It was during a quiet time that I met my mentor, Wilf Chadwick, who worked as a store man at our base.

He was a breeder, trainer and competitor with his German shepherd dogs; one of the top working dog men in the country. I met him over a beer one day, we talked dogs, at least he did, and I just sat and listened. He invited me to his kennels at the weekend. So Saturday mornings off I went. The dogs and the training was a joy to watch. He took me to a working trial to see what happens. I caught the bug.

I had to do this somehow, but I could not have my own dog in barracks, so Wilf gave me one of his to work with. Every weekend I worked the dog. When I got longer leaves, Wilf's wife let me stay in her spare room. Over the next few years I learnt so much from Wilf. From a novice dog handler to a competitor in the top levels of working trials. I was introduced to the top handlers, trainers and judges in the sport, always as the soldier who could not have his own dog. People like Brigadier Campbell, president of the working trials committee of the British Kennel Club. Mrs. Daphne Foreman, the top lady in the sport, they all helped me so much. As long as I live I shall ever be grateful to Wilf Chadwick.

In Britain during 1945 to the 1970's, there were basically two major types of competition for working dogs.

THE BASIC OBEDIENCE TESTS AND THE WORKING TRIALS

Both demanded a high quality of performances, discipline and sportsmanship.

Obedience was carried out in both large halls and fenced outdoor rings, rain or shine. Working trials were always outdoors and required large areas to work in.

At this point I should like to make very clear, especially for the enlightenment of the Board of the Canadian Kennel Club that there is a huge difference between Working Trials and the Schutzhund Sport.

To qualify in the three main tests in Schutzhund, the dog MUST carry out protection work, i.e. search, apprehend and escort a criminal decoy. There is no option, protection test or no Schutzhund entry.

In the Working Trials, that has been regulated and recognized by the Kennel Club in the UK for well over 80 years, do NOT require protection work except in ONE class. The other four classes are obedience, agility, nose work and very disciplined working.

With the difference, those handlers who would like to get away from the automated clockwork obedience tests, but do not wish to train dogs for protection work can not do so. The CKC only recognizes Schutzhund titles, BUT, does not publish a rule book. After over 30 years of discussions by so many different boards and committees of the CKC, they still can not recognize a sport in which hundreds of dogs enter and enjoy in the UK every weekend. More about the CKC in a later chapter, much more!!

However, that's where I started my working life with dogs. There are four elements in the working trial tests; strict, accurate heel work at fast, normal and slow pace. Left and right turns as well as left about and right about turns; extensive long distance send aways and re directions at a distance of 100 meters. Fast and accurate recalls; plus on and off lead work in a group of at least six people. There are also the "speak" on command test and a food refusal test.

The agility work is simple, a long jump, a hurdle jump and an "A" frame to climb.

Nose work and retrieve are tested by dumbbell on flat and over hurdle. Scent ability is carried out in an area which articles are placed. Each article must be no larger than a match box or longer than 6 inches. The dog is sent in to find and retrieve on a timed basis.

These are some of the challenges for the working trial trainer and dog. In the appendix you will find the official tests and scoring.

So "Jinx" and I started to train for the working trials; it was not easy, patience, patience. We did however make progress under the instruction of Wilf. It was not all work however; we also had a lot of fun.

One incident that still makes me smile happened as we were just out for a walk in the woods one evening. Jinx was running around sniffing and playing free like all dogs do, or should do. Suddenly I heard him barking like mad, he sounded serious, I ran and found him. He was standing on the hood of a car barking at the windshield, as I got closer I saw what had attracted him to get excited. Inside the car two young love birds were hastily trying to cover themselves up. Whoops! I called Jinx off and quickly went on my way. It must have been quite a shock for the occupants. I hope it did not spoil their day.

I decided to join the leading club in the UK, the ASPADS. Better known as the Association of Sheep Police and Army Dogs Society; this club organized working trials all over the UK, England, Scotland, Wales and Ireland. They published a good magazine as well. All was going well when disaster struck. The Para's were sent to Egypt to a problem. I had to leave Jinx. Things were quite hot in Egypt for a while, when it all settled down we expected to go back to the UK. No, it did not happen as we were kept in the Middle East as watch dogs.

It was not hard, just boring, patrols, parades and exercises. I took advantage of the night school that the army educational people had set up. I took classes for history, geography and current affairs. My basic education during the war had left much to be desired. I did need an army first class certificate if I was going to get promoted to a senior rank, so I worked. It helped to pass the time and after the examinations it was well worth the effort.

I still had my duties to do, like being on guard of the perimeter of the camp each week. One night while patrolling my area, a small dog began to follow me; I played with him, and swiped some food from the cookhouse and fed him. He became attached to me and even more important to my mates, he became the section mascot. Officers did not mind, some of them had pet dogs.

I taught the dog, who we named "PI" short for "Pihard" or wild dog. He would sit, stay, come, etc. But most important, he became our "detector" dog. When we took him on guard duty with us, he would bark if there was anyone around; this was very handy. If I wanted to sit down, maybe have a forbidden smoke, the "PI" would warn me if the duty officer or the guard sergeant came out to check on us. PI did this for our section, but not for anyone else who did not live in our barrack. There was an amazing coincidence, forty years later one of my students was a Colonel in the Royal Canadian Engineers, Jim Murphy, he was send to Egypt with a UN force. He was based in Ismailia, in Moascar camp. That was where I had been years before. Jim picked up a stray dog and trained it in his spare time. The photo shows him with the dog. I wished I had a picture of PI as well. Even on active service I could at least have some dog around.

THE DOG THAT FLEW AND LOVED IT

One of our young officers had read a book about dogs that the Russians had parachuted during the war; he asked me if it was possible to train his Black Labrador to jump. I told him of course it was, dogs will do anything if we humans are smart enough to show them how. The officer seemed serious; what do we need beside the dog he asked.

I asked him why he wanted his dog to jump. His reply did seem to make sense.

I would like to teach the dog to find injured men on the landing zone, at the moment we have to send soldiers out to search the area; this is very difficult at night. It would help if the dog could find the man and bark or get our attention in some way. It could save lives.

The first thing we did was to take the dog up for flights to acclimatize him to the aircraft, the noise and the movements did not worry the dog one iota, he loved the rides.

The next stage was to design a comfortable harness that was safe for the dog, so a harness of webbing and hooks was made; again the dog thought it was great fun being swung around in the contraption.

Now what about a parachute, the officer had friends in the Air Dispatch Section and suddenly a small cargo chute arrived out of the blue; of course, no one knew where it had come from???

Now we really got busy, we made up a dummy dog and proceeded to throw it out of the aircraft a few times, it worked.

The day of the big test, we used a helicopter to make it simple and easier to control. Up went the officer and his dog. At about 600 feet out came the dog, followed by his master. We were all spread out on the ground, ready for the worst. The chute deployed, the dog floated down, barking all the time, he landed well and was so excited.

Our efforts must have come to the attention of the senior high ups, the project was stopped. We were told that if the idiot animal welfare clowns found out, there would be hell to pay with the publicity.

So the jumping search dog ceased to exist, officially.

I can assure that the dog went on to make at least eight jumps and was awarded his wings as a qualified parachutist.....but it was fun doing it..............................

Duty in Egypt over and back to England; go on leave have fun, meet the girls, and whoa meet the girls!! Well it happened I met a girl that I had known years ago. Anyway, it happened. We were engaged, met my mother, who had forgiven me for all my past deeds, I think. We were married, and moved into an Army Married Quarter. Very soon I was back to Wilf's kennel, with wife in tow. She was not interested in dogs; could that have been a serious mistake? Jinx was glad to see me and we just carried on where we had stopped. Once day Wilf said it's about time you entered a title trial. We did Most of the tests went fairly well but the "eagle" was not there. Wilf told me now you have a wife and a house you need a dig. I agreed but I said I think the problem will be the wife. He told me not to worry. Over the next few weeks while training with Jinx, I noticed that Wilf's wife kept taking my wife to the house. Even Wilf paid more attention to her than he did not me. Soon I realized why. On the way home one day my wife surprised me by saying why don't we have Jinx over to our place? Crafty Wilf, he and his wife had "brain washed my wife to think it was her idea to have Jinx permanently. I got the idea and grudgingly agreed to have the dog at home. Whoopi!

From then on it was so much fun, with one exception. While playing with Jinx in our living room my wife hid behind the chesterfield. Jinx jumped over it and landed on her foot, breaking the wife's toe. I told her the dog would have to go back. She flew into a temper and said it was my fault not the dogs. He is not going back. Strange how some things workout. Another, what I consider was a piece of good luck was the fact that I was promoted to a senior rank and was to be posted my own squadron in Ripon, Yorkshire BUT NOT out on the moors.

At this time we had a wonderful daughter, Linda, so I went to Ripon to see the situation. Beautiful town, nice new open barracks and better still nice new married quarters with big gardens.

I checked to find out how long it would before a house was available, the news was not good. There was a three months waiting list. Nothing attempted, nothing gained so I found the person who was in charge of the house allocations. Quite by chance of course I found myself standing beside the very man in his local pub. A few beers later, quite a few, the subject of a house came up in our conversation. I managed to impress upon him the vital need for a nice large house with a garden and near some open fields. Thank goodness he was a dog lover. Within two days there became available a house in a nice position. So unexpected!! Call to the wife, tell her to get moving. Few days later it was all done, home sweet home. We were now living deep in sheep country; I knew from my boyhood just what damage a rogue dog could wreck on a flock of sheep, I had to be absolutely sure that Jinx was proofed against sheep worrying. Ripon cattle market was held each week in the city, I started to go down with Jinx. We would wander around the sheep pens and generally get him used to the smells and the movements of the sheep. When questioned by one of the farmers, I told him what I was doing. He said he wished more people would think like me. He allowed me to put the dog into a pen with the sheep, he sniffed and stood back, I told him to sit and down in the pen, if he moved I gave him a hard voice correction. Soon all the farmers knew me and what I was doing. We often would go for a beer together. I mentioned that I liked to do tracking across the fields; the area farmers gave me their permission to use their fields at any time. One farmer's son became interested and he would lay tracks for us.

Jinx was getting well known in the city, people would stop me and talk about him. One teacher asked me if I would take him to her school and talk to the children. It was fun. We would talk about dogs, why children should not touch stray dogs and if an adult was with the dog always ask before you pet the dog. Then the fun tricks. I had a signal to make him bark once, so I asked the children what was 2 +2, and then I would ask Jinx if the child was right and he would bark 4 times. I put a dog treat on his nose and he had to wait until I told him to catch it. We did lots of tricks and the children were great. We were called to the school one day and the children presented Jinx with a dog coat with his name embroidered on it. The made him the school mascot. This meant we had to attend on prize days and other school events.

One thing I missed from down south was the training on Sunday mornings with other club members. In UK there are so many co-operations with police dogs and their handlers. We all worked together training and all entered the working trials together. The nearest police dog was based over twenty miles away from Ripon, so we could not get together very often. This does not happen in general in North America. For some reason the police chiefs do not allow mixing of their dogs either in training or competition. One reason is the lack of control and discipline of the police dogs when "off lead". The other reason is the attitude that a dog in police service must be so tough when arresting a criminal.

Years later, I witnessed a most disgusting display by Ontario Provincial Police dogs and their handlers. And this was a demonstration at the National Schutzhund trial. A decoy criminal ran away and an officer sent the dog to stop him, the dog did indeed stop the criminal and was biting indiscriminately all over the padded suit, including the legs, even while he was on the ground. That was bad enough, but what followed was disgusting. It took <u>THREE</u> officers to get the dog off the criminal. All day we had watched the Schutzhund dogs release if the criminal stood still. If there was no agitation by the criminal there was no need to hold and bite.

The Schutzhund left instantly when the handler gave the command to leave. The macho attitude of many North American police handlers is disgraceful. A real live criminal does not have massive padded protection. A dog can savage an unprotected person and inflict serious injury. If the police officers are so tough, then let them run with no padded arms. I don't think so.

To teach a dog protection work is not difficult, to the dog it is natural to chase and bite. It is the control that counts. The skill is to train a dog to chase <u>BUT</u> stop on command, even before he reaches the criminal. That's the way the protection work is taught and tested in the Working Trials. Even a criminal does not deserve to be ripped up by a dog out of control.

My friends tell me that now the RCMP dogs are trained to the "call off" command. What if the criminal is not the criminal but the passerby? A dog is not a weapon; it is a tool to be used as carefully as a gun and a taser projector.

Life went on, training and tracking; I built a six foot wooden scale wall in the back yard. Jinx soon was able to climb up and carefully come down the other side. The wall was an obstacle at the working trials way back when. Now it has been replaced by the "A" frame, easier on the dog's shoulders when landing.

The next adventure was just that, an adventure. It was the habit of the local farm lads to come into the city on Saturday nights for a few beers and to have some harmless fun. Maybe go on to the dance at the city hall, they were a nice bunch of lads; never caused any real trouble just mischief and a bit of noise. One evening the lads were in the dance, a bunch of riff-raff and hard cases from Leeds decided to pay the city a visit. They just had to tease and upset the local lads. The obvious happened. The idiots from Leeds got to real good hiding and were thrown out and chased from the city. The Leeds mob were not prepared to leave it at that, they challenged the locals to a real bundle in the square the following Saturday night. It did seem as if there was going to be serious trouble. The local Constable knew what was going on and decided that it had to be stopped before it got out of hand and really bad. He had arranged for assistance from the County Police, this included two police dogs and their handlers. The constable came to my house to ask if I would turn out with Jinx. I told him we had only just started protection work. Not to worry, he replied, I just want the dogs to be seen and that should be enough to deter the hot heads.

So the following Saturday Jinx and I were at the police station being briefed by the Inspector in charge of the event. The plan was simple in design, the extra police would be kept out of sight in their vans, the Inspector would warn the trouble makers to stop and go home. His object was to keep the two groups apart. If that did not work, the police would seal all roads in to the square and contain the whole group. The dogs were only to come out if the situation demanded a stern reaction. I was to keep with the police handlers and do what they told me to do.

Things did not go to well at the start, the Inspector was knocked down, so the road blocks went up and the extra police moved in to the square. The dogs were called forward, we walked in a line towards the shouting youths, the dogs started to bark and get excited. Jinx took a look and joined in just as fierce as the other dogs. The mob took one look at the line of dogs and moved back. One road was opened to allow the crowd out a few at a time. They went to their cars and drove away. Within half an hour it was all over, the idiots that assaulted the Inspector were arrested with no problems. Off they went to the clink. We all relaxed and the police handlers talked to me abut Jinx reactions, they said they were impressed by this size and his courage in the noise and crowd. So was I.

One of the handlers told me if I could get over to the county police HQ, he would help me with the protection work, for a dog not fully trained he showed that he has the guts to make a fine working dog. A few weeks later I received a letter of thanks from the Inspector and a nice new tracking harness as a gift from the handlers. On Sunday I called Wilf and told him, he was pleased and said "now Jinx is yours, I will transfer his Kennel Club papers to you".

You must join our coach party to "Crufts".

This sounded more like a command than an invitation, but once the magic word "Crufts" was mentioned, all the other voices joined in the chorus. "Oh you must come to "Crufts". This I knew was a dog beauty show in London that was the full extent of my knowledge. These people were the local dog club members in Ripon; I used to go to watch the dogs being put through their paces. I helped out with odd jobs. Then this "mass hysteria" broke out and it seemed that nothing on earth would or could prevent me going on an outing to "Crufts".

On a very cold morning at 4am on a February dawn I clambered aboard the club coach, leaving my family warm in bed. Feeling cold and hungry for there was no time to cook breakfast, and my wife was dead to the world.

I wondered if I was completely in sane, suffering all this pain and discomfort just for a dog show. The coach stopped at intervals to pick up more frozen people and their dogs of all shapes, sizes and colors. I found myself sharing the seat with a huge Great Dane, who did not look too pleased at being dragged out from his cozy kennel, so we consoled each other and tried to get some sleep. Who do you think will get a ticket today? One member queried at no one in particular.

Good grief, I thought, surely we will all be able to get admission tickets, and voiced this to another member, who promptly burst out laughing. There was a roar of hilarity from the other passengers when told of my remark, and they all proceeded to put me in the picture explaining that the "tickets" were the Kennel Club Challenge Certificates awarded for the best of breed in each breed of dog, a much prized reward.

I began to catch all the excitement that everyone was feeling, and this mounted to fever pitch as the coach arrived at the Olympia. A stern young policeman opened the door and informed us all very loudly, "you have one minute to unload, or the driver will be done for obstructing traffic".

Over thirty people with dogs, bags, coats and equipment were quickly deposited on the sidewalk. As it was still only 7:30am and I was by now feeling ravenous, I decided to go in search of food. Finding a small café behind Olympia, I slid into the warmth. "Just off a dog coach, enquired the man behind the counter?" I nodded and pleaded for tea and bacon sandwiches. "Where you from?" asked a lady trying to hide a big Boxer dog under the table. Ripon I replied, and was informed that she had travelled all night from Scotland. Slowly I was realizing that this was no ordinary dog show, and by the time my meal was over I had talked to people from all over the country. As I arrived at one of the gates of the hall, I was literally run into by a lady trying to manage four very boisterous Golden Retrievers. Can I help? I asked and was rewarded with a beam of relief. Take these two, will you, while I get sorted out. I held them while she found her pass and entry cards. Come on she said, I have an extra pass you can have, and off we went to the exhibitor's entrance gate.

I was rendered speechless by the sight of an absolute rugby scrum of dogs and people milling around and getting into lines, at the head of which were a series of ramps. Vets in white coats were standing beside the ramps, and one reached out for the dogs I was holding.

"Quick, urged the lady" get them through for me, here's your pass and the dogs numbers. The vet surveyed the dogs, looked closely at both ends, lifted up the tail and said mechanically, OK next please. I was through, what do I do now as the lady was nowhere to be seen. The crowd seemed to be flowing up the side of the hall; then exploding into the main arena which was full of wooden pens upon which some dogs were lying.

"Up the top on the right" shouted a stout red faced vicar, who was being towed along at high speed by two large Rottweilers. I decided to take his advice as he did seem to know the routine. "What's your bench number mate" called out a cheerful cockney man. 4453, 4454, I replied. You're next to me then the cockney informed me. I explained that these were not my dogs and I was beginning to get worried, when the owner arrived, complete with bags and the other two dogs. After a few minutes of chaos, the correct dogs were secured on the correct benches and I was free to look around. For a while I just wandered around, taking in the atmosphere, seeing hundreds of varied breeds and dogs I had never seen before, I also watched the obedience work, it was excellent, so smooth and accurate. Then it was time to look for my favorite breed. I enquired from a passing doggy lady if she knew where the German shepherd dogs were. "Shepherd What?" she said "I am in MinPoos myself" My sense of humor was touched, visualizing this lady, who was over six feet tall and must have weighed over 250 pounds, being with a miniature poodle.

At last I found the Shepherds, meeting and being introduced to others as the soldier with one of Wilf Chadwick's dogs. An unexpected sight was the many stalls, displaying every know kind of dog food, veterinary products and beauty preparations. There were dog portraits, coats, aprons and everything for dogs in the world. The highlight of the day was when the Supreme Champion was chosen. The audience sat or stood in an electric silence while the tension mounted as the dogs were paraded, and the roar of the crowd was deafening. The day had passed so quickly and it was time to find the coach. The club members were in high spirits, two having gained a Challenge Certificate and others being well placed as well. Those that did not have a good day were philosophical about it. Oh well, there is always next year. After midnight I staggered home, exhausted but very happy and having learnt so much about the dog game.

I thought that I would be in Ripon for at least three years, that was the normal for most senior non commissioned officers, but the Commanding Officer called me for an interview. He said, "I don't know if it is good news or bad, but you are off to Cyprus again. Somehow there has been a switch in posting; it is a strangest one that I have never seen before. You are replacing a man who is not going because he has a compassionate posting due to family illness. Maybe that's the bad news; the strange part is that you are not going to an army unit. I said I do not understand. He continued, you are going to Cyprus Police as an explosive expert. The Colonial Office has arranged it. The better news is that it is only for six months. That was it. My wife was furious. There was nothing I could do. A week later I was in Cyprus at "Athlasa" police station, part of an emergency police reserve unit. The commander was a British Police Inspector and all the constables were Turkish. I had not got a clue what I was supposed to do; at least all the Turkish lads spoke English. My room was nice, the food was good. After I settled in I was told my duties, simply deal with explosive items that were found or left to cause problems. The group was a "mobile reserve". That meant no police traffic duties just 24 hours stand by for trouble. Doing nothing meant boredom. I started to lecture the group on explosive problems, basically "don't touch" what more could I do. I exercised to keep fit, I went on the range to practice pistol shooting, the lads taught me self defense. On duty all the time but nothing to do; I cursed the damn job. While walking around the area one day I discovered the police dog kennels. All the dogs except one were German Shepherds. The odd one was a black Labrador retriever. He was just in a kennel doing nothing, like me. I found out that the dog had been sent up from South Africa as a tracking and search dog but there should have been a handler with it. All the Cyprus police dogs were patrol and arrest dogs, none were trained to work a tracking dog. I began to show the dog handlers how to lay tracks and get the dog working again, for me it was fun, but a senior officer suggested that it would only make sense for me to take over the dog. I think that he really meant that as I did not have much to do, I should make myself useful. This suited me fine. "Mick", as the dog was called, was a good tracking dog. I thought back to the lessons that Wilf had taught me, not only tracking but to carry out effective searches of grounds and buildings. I managed to get him to find things I had buried and obviously any type of explosives.

There was a little problem in Cyprus at the time. Some of the EOKA terrorists were getting very cunning, they would go on a raid or ambush them instead of taking their weapons and equipment home, they would hide them in holes dug in the fields. It was decided to mount some searches around the villages that were suspected of being EOKA homes. The answer was to use the dog. The areas we were to search were large. Another problem was that the soldiers who first searched the area would ruin any tracks and scent. We arrived one morning in an area of grape vines and other crops.

I put Mick into harness and started to cover the area; it was a waste of time, so many scents of soldiers or farmers. So I took him off harness and let him run loose using just the voice encouraging to "find it". I did not hold many hopes for luck.

Suddenly he began to sniff and scratch at a patch of vines, I went over for a look and he began to get excited and started to bark, as I looked he pulled out a piece of raffia material. I gave it a pull and realized it was a big lid of basket, in front of me was now a big hole in the ground about three feet wide. I began to worry, there must be something in there; was it a booby trap? Inside of the holes could see a blanket, so feeling very up tight, I attached a string to it and got every one back out of the way. Slowly I pulled the string; the blanket came out, nothing happened. Creeping back and looking into the hole, I saw there were weapons in the bottom.

We pulled out two rifles, a sub machine gun (American) and some grenades. There were also washing and shaving items and some shirts and pants. That was it. "Mick" had done it without my help; I was so pleased and proud of him. He had proven that there were uses for dogs in the search missions. On return to the police station "Mick" was over petted, over fed and overjoyed at all the attention, he even got a pat on the head from the Chief Constable's lady wife. Dog back to the kennel and a clean up myself, then over to the police canteen.

The celebrations started; these young Turkish boys knew how to celebrate. Singing and dancing, it was so much fun. The Turkish brandy was no real problem, it was the way we drank it by the glass full. Anyways, someone put me to bed; in the morning it was terrible, I had two heads, both of them spinning and dizzy. Beware of

Turks and brandy. Life went on, practice with "Mick", eat, sleep, and drink. Then another job, this time to search some buildings in a small village in the Trodos mountain area. All the men between16 and 60 had been rounded up by the Army for questioning. The constables, the dog and I started to search the buildings for weapons. Check the floors and walls, etc.

One of the young Turks found a small hole in a wall; he said there was another wall behind it. I brought "Mick" in, he sniffed and barked and began to scratch the wall. We dug at it, the wall soon came down, and guess what, two men were dragged out. We checked the photo book and sure enough they were both wanted terrorists. They were not worried about us, but they sure did not like the dog. Another day over and back to the base. I was really worried about the "celebrations" that would follow that evening. It was right for me to worry. Same brandy, same hangover. My six months with the police was nearly over, in some ways I wanted to stay in Cyprus, but I also wanted to go home to the family and "Jinx". The day came. The Chief Constable thanked me and said "Times up".

The lads gave me a huge party; I do not remember much of it. I do remember having to go down to the kennel to say goodbye to "Mick". So I cried, it was tough, but I knew his young Turk handler would look after him.

I will never forget "Mick" and all that he did for me, work wise and personally.

As all military people know, we just get settled down with a unit, in a town, and the army will decide to move you to a new town, about every three years on average. My luck was out again. I was posted to Germany. This was the last straw for my wife. With my daughter and a new son she refused to travel again. She went back to her family. Germany, the nation with the best working dogs in the world. At least there was a small silver lining in the huge black family cloud.

The Squadron I was sent to consisted mainly of Nation Service men, i.e. young men called up for two years compulsory army service.

The Sergeant Major I took over from told me there were discipline problems. For these young men, with nothing much to do at nights and the weekends, it was not surprising. With the help of the officers we organized "Adventure" trips. Groups were taken to the plants where Volks Wagons were made and also Mercedes. These went well so they were expanded. Groups went to Austria to Ski or to Denmark for camping. We always tried to do a little military training, but it was the change of atmosphere that helped to solve the problems. We played football with the local German teams, and some men took up canoeing with the local club. Gradually things got better, and there were fewer absentees or drunk problems. My efforts were to hook up with the nearby "Schutzhund" club. I went and watched them training and began to be accepted as a "dog man". I learnt so much in those sessions. The big day was when the local trials were held. I was so happy to be asked to be one of the helpers. With a full padded suit, I got to know the power of the dogs and the skill of the handlers. I also did enjoy the huge party afterwards. Most important was to see the sportsmanship and comradeship between all the members.

ON MILITARY EXERCISES AGAIN

"HALT STILLE", a light flashed in my face, I halted and stood very still. I am a British soldier, I called out. The voice in the dark replied "stand still until I bring my dog up to meet you". In the spread of his flash light I saw a great black beast with the head of an ox. It was a Rottweiler. Are you lost said the policeman on the end of the dogs lead. No, I am trying not to get caught by the other soldiers in the forest.

I had an easy time so far, it had been no problem to get into the enemy camp, find the tent of the Commanding Officer, steal his maps and note books and get away with out being seen. Now I had to get back to our rendezvous to hand over my loot to another officer.

Everything had gone so well until the "HALT STILLE". You can relax now the officer told me; we are on your side for these exercises. I will take you in my patrol car to join two other soldiers. His small car took me to the next town a few kilometers away. I did not really relax on this ride as the dog was sitting on the back seat behind me, breathing hot breath on the back of my neck. In perfect English the officer said, "my dogs name is "KARL" he goes everywhere with me and it's a very good dog". I took his word for that, I had to.

At the police station I met the other lads. "What do we do now?" I asked. "Just wait for an officer to come and pick up the proceeds of our raids". I asked the officers there, "Where has KARL gone". Back on patrol they said. I told them about my "arrest" and that I did not try to run. Good job, said the officer, KARL is the best police dog in North Saxony, and you would not have got very far. He has the most arrests of all our dogs. The police officers fed us and I drifted off to sleep after nearly two days running around the forest playing soldiers.

"Would you like some coffee?" said a voice and KARL's owner was beside me, "I have to write my reports then I can go home". "How about introducing me to your dog" I asked. He called the dog over. I realized that although I was sitting on a chair, his dog's shoulders were level with my waist. I could not get over his size, yet one word from his master and he was so obedient. There did seem to be a secret understanding between dog and man. "My name is Rudi" he said, "what is yours?"

"Art" I replied. "Tell me more about your dog". He explained so much about the breeding, training and working of the Rottweiler. I told him about "Jinx" and what I hoped to do with him, make him a working trial champion. We exchanged addresses and he went home.

I wondered when I would ever see another Rottweiler. One thing about life in the army is that you never know what is going to happen next.

The British Government decided to cut back on the troops in Germany, so here came another move, not only a move back to England, but the break up of my squadron, mainly as National Service was going to be halted, no more two year men.

I was sent to the training regiment, Oh there is a good God somewhere as it was only five miles from Wilf Chadwick's place, plus there was a nice semi-detached house that was ready for me. Now to persuade my wife to come with the children. She agreed and it looked as if a normal life would be possible. Wife, kids and dog, all near Wilf. Life in a training regiment is good for most staff. The place is run on a five day week; the hours are usually 8 am to 4 pm with very few duty weekends. I was happy to go along with this. I told my wife about the Rottweiler "KARL" she said why not look for a breeder near to us and go and see the dogs. The Kennel Club gave me the address of a breeder, Mrs. Mary McPhail. She was only a few miles away so I wrote to ask if we could come to see the dogs. She answered, come over when you can. Kids and dog loaded into my van and off we went. Mrs. McPhail greeted us and after a coffee, we went out to the kennel to se some puppies; seven tiny six week old bundles of fluff. As we were driving home my wife surprised me by saying, we had one dog another will not make much difference. It was decided. As I was in my last four years of service, I did not expect to be sent overseas again, or even moved from the unit at all.

So the second dog arrived. All the puppy work started, socializing the puppy as well as feeding, cleaning, and exercise. The two am trips to the piddle routine as well. Training and trialing continued with Jinx and we began to do very well at the working trials. After working a trial near London, I was approached by a real gentlemen, Rolls Royce and all that stuff. "Do you ever do private security jobs with your dog?" he asked. He also explained that his daughters wedding reception was to be held at his house in the country, and like "Jinx" and I to help with the security, it would be for two days, just guarding the house and property. I knew I would be on leave at the time so I accepted. It would be experience for Jinx and a few shillings for me. I also thought that if it worked well it might be an option for when I left the army, as no one could live on an army pensions. One Friday afternoon I arrived at Mr. Cohen's house, or mansion as it looked to me. It was a massive property surrounded by a high wall with large entrance gates, all lawns and flower gardens; I was very impressed how tidy it was.

I was met by a gentleman who introduced himself as Mr. Cohen's private secretary, we went into a large office and he offered me a drink, I said coffee would be good. A nice maid brought the coffee and looking at "Jinx" she asked if he would like something to eat. Maybe she thought he looked hungry, anyway I explained that he only ate at the night time and that he was never allowed to accept food from strangers. (This of course was one of the tests at the trials, food refusal) I saw she wanted to make friends with the dog, so I said come and meet him, stroke him; he is a nice friendly dog with friends.

The wedding was a high society affair with two of the richest families being involved. There were many guests bringing with them lots of valuable gifts and possessions, jewelry, etc. Mr. Cohen had insisted that a large room be set aside to display all the wedding gifts so that they could be viewed by everyone. What an attractive target for the league of light fingered men. He had hired a guard to be in the room at all times. I wished the guard could be armed, but British law does not allow it.

The secretary was very worried about any gate crashers, who might try to get in. That was why Jinx and I would look after the outside area. There was also a possible problem from press and media types. Some press had been invited, but the fear was that some free lancers and the gutter press would try to get in. The local police would take care of the outside of the property and the traffic control.

I was given very clear instructions, to patrol the grounds, watch the walls and if there were problems at the gate I was to help there. Off I went to walk the complete area, looking for obvious points of entry, trees over hanging the wall or to see if someone had left a ladder nearby. I planned my patrol routes for night keeping an eye on a small lean tool shed near the wall; it might not help someone to get in, but sure would make it fast and easy to get out. I was able to speak to the head gardener and warn him and his men not to wander about in the dark, and if told to stand still, do it, or the dog might get ideas, he has 42 teeth and may apply them to anyone's backside if they did not freeze.

I got ready for my patrol taking a leash, flashlight and a good heavy baton. At 11:30 pm an alarm came from the main gate; I went over and stood in the shadows watching the gate keepers arguing with a man. I came out of the dark, told Jinx to bark and the man decided to go away. He was a reporter who wanted to talk to Mr. Cohen. After an offer of a thick ear from the gate keeper and Jinx's advice, he just went, smart fellow.

Just after midnight "jinx" began to growl and get restless, he led me to an area by the wall and I saw a man slipping over; I waited until he was well over and then shone the light on him. I said "Stand still, do not move". To my surprise, he did. With jinx watching close, I searched the man, he had a few tools on him. Then we went to the main gate. The police were there, so I handed him and his tools over. I asked him why he had not made a run for it, he replied, "Not bloody likely, the last time I ran I got bitten by a dog". I made a short statement and got back on patrol, very pleased as to what Jinx had done for me. No more alarms. I was ready for breakfast and a rest when daylight came. Saturday was the big day, from early morning guests were arriving. I kept out of the way, but kept my eyes open. I was asked to stand in for the gift room guard to allow him to get a meal.

All the presents had been set out in a huge room; the tables were covered with silver, jewellery and some paintings, it was fabulous and must have been worth millions of pounds. Soon after I settled in, a very well dressed man came to the door and said he wanted to see the gifts. I told him I was very sorry but he could not come in the room. He did seem very upset, but after looking at Jinx, who was eying him up, he just went away. Soon he was back, this time with Mr. Cohen. He had made a complaint that I would not let him into the room.

Mr. Cohen told him that it was my duty to keep everyone out and that I had been quite correct. I was told that the man was the groom's father and that I had stopped one of the richest men in the world. The man did laugh and said to me "It is easier to get into my diamond offices than to try to get in here". He also said "Thank you for being so polite when you threw me out". They both shook my hand and that was it; I was relieved by a guard and went back outside.

Back at the main gate, all was calm and quiet, just a few reporters but no problems. In fact, we gave them a cup of tea. Then came a little bit of bother; no one had told us that the groom was from South Africa, if they had we might have been ready for the next stage.

By cars and coaches a large number of students arrived. They were here to protest the South African political "Apartheid". The police dealt with most of them, but a small group of three students climbed over the wall; I sent Jinx towards them, and told them to stop. Two did, one hero ran across the lawn towards the house, Jinx tripped him up but he did not bite. I grabbed the youth, who was swearing at me, but only when he saw the press reporters did he shout, "The dog has ripped me". At the gate, in front of everyone, I told the idiot to show us the blood. There was none, so everyone burst out laughing at the fool. Then he took a kick at me and suddenly found a German shepherd holding his arm, very tightly. I told Jinx to leave and the police arrested him.

The next day different newspapers printed very different reports and photographs.

One showed the student holding his arm with Jinx next to him. Another paper published a photo of Jinx sitting with bride's maids and small pages being hugged by the bride. Such a vicious dog!! There is no limit to what some papers will print just to get sales. Like most people today I read them for entertainment, certainly not for truth and enlightenment.

The job was over. I received a generous tip from the groom and an excellent cheque from Mr. Cohen. Maybe security might be my next job after my service was over.

Life went on. I joined the local dog club. They were all working dogs, i.e. obedience, tracking and now with Jinx and the Rottweiler "Dera" also working trials. Wednesday evening we all practices the obedience routines, Sunday mornings out in the fields we tracked the dogs and put them through the working trial exercises. It was such fun, everyone helped each other, especially the Kent County Police dog handlers, and we all worked to train and also enter the competitions.

The British Kennel Club had organized a national trained dog reserve. The dogs would track and search under the police supervision. When considered competent, the dogs and owners would be tested; this included first aid, map reading and communications. It was quite a difficult test and took a full weekend to cover. An interesting off shoot of the VTDR was a few visits to the airport to get the dogs used to rides in a helicopter. They did not mind the noise, and were eager to hop into the aircraft. The important thing in most of Europe was the co-operation between civilians, police and all the various rescue services. This was not general in North America as I found out later in my life with dogs. Late one night we were awakened by a very determined hammering at my front door. Not in one of my best moods, I went down, telling the dogs to shut up. Opening the door I was surprised to see a police sergeant and another gentlemen standing there. I invited them in and waited for an explanation for the 3 am visit. This man is the father of a ten year old girl who did not arrive home from school today. She has been missing since this afternoon and we have come to ask you and all the VTDR members to come and help with a search. "Give me ten minutes to get dressed", I told them. My wife had come downstairs and she took off to make a flask of coffee for me. It was a matter of honor that all VTDR would turn out at any time to help.

My wife phoned a few members and I picked them up in my van and went to the search headquarters. We were briefed as to our area and soon were out ready to start.

The business of searching is a very serious affair; if the searches do not get organized, they can get into all sorts of trouble, including getting lost or worse. Training and preparation is vital. In my van I always kept what I called my panic kit, first aid kit, maps and suitable weather apparel, rubber boots, hat and rain coat. We knew the search area quite well; there were some bad spots; a tidal river, old pits and quarries, plus plenty of wooded areas. It was not the first time that a child had got lost around this area. The police control point was set up in large trailer. We received our final briefing on the spot. The girl had left school with a group of other children, this day she had branched off and gone her own way. She had not been seen since four o'clock, the parents waited before going out to look for her, and then put in a 999 emergency call. Now it was three hours since she left the other children and soon it would be dark. Two dog teams were detailed to search the bank of the river. Dera and I with other teams were sent with police lines through the woods. We checked through the area slowly and carefully, the roads and ditches, paths and some old buildings at disused quarries where a child might hide or go to sleep. The dogs were both surface tracking and wind scenting. As darkness fell we had nothing. Midnight we were all called to the control point where the senior police officer had to call off the search, we would start again at day light. Get food and rest; be ready for an early start.

The local army camp provided food, showers and cots for us, no one wanted to talk very much, in our minds was the fear for the little girl. Imagination is most upsetting when thoughts lead to kidnapping, assault or even death; no one slept much either. Up before dawn, washed and fed and ready to go again. More searchers had arrived so the whole area was swept again. A report came that the girl's school bag had been found by one of the police officers. We worked harder, carefully under bushes and any place that could hide a child. At four the search was called off, we were told to stand down. The girl had been found dead. She had fallen over the edge of a quarry pit hole and the fallen debris covered her body. Soldiers who were digging all the fresh earth falls and disturbances had found her. We all dispersed and went home, feeling so disappointed at the tragic outcome. For weeks afterwards I would look at my family and think of the terrible things that could happen even in the best of regulated homes.

Searches like this can be soul destroying and frustrating, but if the need arises there are always plenty of people who will turn out to help. Even people with pet dogs can help if they will agree to take a little training. Remember, it does not need a dog with a mile long pedigree to become a useful search dog.

There were good times as well, in training and at the trials. I have just remembered where and how I received my first dog bite. It had been a good weekend trial, nice weather, good tracking fields and big crowds to watch the obedience and agility on the Sunday afternoon. Most of the dogs qualified and so we celebrated in the local pub; just a few beers. Time came to go to our homes and to say our good byes to friends. I had "Dera" on leash beside me, my fiend from Scotland had his police dog beside him, normal as we went to shake hands, maybe a little unsteady, his dog bit my hand and Dera bit his. After the shock, we both burst out laughing. At every trial after that people would say to me "Hello Art, I won't shake hands, and how is your hand?" Neither of us ever lived that down. Motto, "hey stupid", don't drink much with a dog beside you.

Another little incident that I have to smile at from the past; my Commanding Officer told me that he was not happy with the dog handlers that patrolled our barracks at night. He said they are scruffy and need a wake up call. So off I went to the kennels. The kennels were clean, the equipment and kitchen was not too bad. I gave the soldiers a talk about looking smart and alert on duty, and then had a look at the dogs. They looked good except one; a big German shepherd whose coat was awful; dry and sticking up all over the place. The handler told me he brushes the dog every day but it makes not difference. I advised him that a spoonful of ordinary cooking oil each day would help to put life into his coat. A week later I went back and the dog was ten times worse. I asked "did you feed him oil daily?" The young lad replied "I thought you meant for me to rub oil on his coat".

Life was very good for me, a nice 8 to 4 job, and no weekend on duty now. I took every opportunity to work any security jobs that came up. Some were "hairy"; some were funny and most were pathetically boring. The local police inspector had recommended me for a job to look after a petrol distribution plant for a Sunday. I took it. When I arrived the manager took me around the site, gave me the keys and said "Good Luck".

Jinx and I patrolled the area, checked the buildings and fences, and looked into all washrooms to make sure that all the water was tuned off. I gave all the safes and lockers a good pull to make sure they were locked. It is amazing how many people forget to lock safes on a Friday night; too busy to get away for the weekend. On empty property the most damage is caused by fire and flooding, but there are always those people who would break in to steal or just cause damage. Vandals are a pain. Late afternoon, Jinx began to get agitated, I could not see why. As I turned a corner I soon did. Two youths about twenty years old were trying to turn the valves of the storage tanks. I shouted and challenged them; they were the usual types of louts that hang about on street corners up to no good.

They turned and gave me lots of advice as to where I should go, and then began to throw rocks and broken glass at me. Jinx was most upset so I let him loose, he went like a bomb and grabbed one youth by his arm, he went down and laid still. The other youth was not so sensible; he ran to the fence and tried to climb over. The nearest part of his anatomy was his backside, to which was soon attached to a large angry German shepherd dog. With Jinx watching, I had no problem escorting them to the gate house and soon the police arrived. The two youths were in a sorry state, one with a bleeding arm, one who would not sit down for a few days. The final outcome of the event was that the two received six months in a young offender's jail. Even thought the Judge knew that both youths have previous criminal records, he proceeded to "Tell me off" for using the dog to make the arrest. The police inspector gave me a pat on the back and put me on to a few more security jobs. It was a good pay day from the owner of the petrol plant as well.

GETTING SERIOUS

Wilf decided that I should work more difficult tracks than the kennel club regulations required. For a KC trial, the Tracking Dog TD title rules are clear. The track is to be a minimum of half a mile long. The track must include at least four turns and three articles are to be laid, and the track must be three hours old. To make it interesting, a cross track by another person must be laid. Any dog that qualified on those requirements must be a good tracking dog.

With the co-operation between the police, search and rescue civilians, Wilf realized that searches would be more difficult, longer and the hours working would be difficult. At first he put me onto older tracks, even up to six hours, then the length of track became up to two or three miles. We had many failures; the long distance was the biggest problem. We developed small ways to help the dog, short rests on the track, a wet cloth to wipe any dust, etc. from the dog's nose and face. We found that at least one long track per week, with a few short ones helped to keep the dog keen and develop his stamina.

Very few people understand the varied situations and conditions that help or hamper a dog while sniffing the scents of a track. A fresh laid track by a human will have "two" scents. One in the air being blown around by the wind and the other locked onto the ground. Obviously the "wind" scent disperses quickly, the ground is a very different matter. What "odors" go into a dog's nose from a foot print on a track?

The crushing earth
The crushing of vegetation
The crushing of insects

These tend to stay long as scent.

Next: Scent of footwear, polish, etc.
Fibers of clothing with layers scent
Body scent, perspiration, spit, etc.
Occupational scents, gas, oil, and for example, the food handlers scent
Soaps, shampoo, aftershave or the residual tobacco scent if a smoker.

There are also differences in various body scents depending on the food diet of an individual, i.e. curry, fish, even candy.

There are also differences in some of the ethnic make up of the body. These are the scents that in one way or another make a definite single scent to a dog. It is proven and tested on all tracks. How? If I knew I could get on my knees and do what the dogs do in a natural way. Just in these few lines you now know that if a criminal would only run away, driving his feet into the ground, getting hot and sweaty, some times stopping for a rest in one spot, it would help the dog, especially if the runner drops a cigarette end or a candy wrapper.

But, it does not usually happen like that. So many other factors must be considered. We will call these the "External Conditions" for the lack of a better name. Heat, wind, light and moisture; these plus temperature must be considered. All these conditions affect humans and can be measured accurately.

Heat: Everyone knows, hot air rises, so will much of the track scent with it.

Wind: Blowing a gale across the track does not help, but a gentle breeze may just move the wind scent over to the side of the actual track contact.

Moisture: Pouring rain can wash out everything; a gentle mist may lock the scent on the ground.

Temperature: Extreme variations will affect the ground. Below -10 degrees and above +90 will not help. So the longer tracks do challenge the dog. Only with practice under similar conditions can the problems be made less difficult.

There are thousands of books and articles as to how a dog can track. How his olfactory nerves in his nose work. Read them. I am interested in the practical work that the dog does. How to help him and what may deter him. Most people interested in starting to track with their dog soon realize that after a certain period, the wind borne scent is gone; also most of the track layers personal scent must have gone. This leaves the ground or track scent lonly. If we start a track while the two scents are there, there must come a point in time when the total becomes only one, the track scent. Will the dog get mixed up if he starts on a mix of ground air suddenly only ground scent remains? Some beginner dogs do have that problem in early training. The handler, MUST, should or could know what the dog's problem is. Do not despair. There is a way to find out when the change is due.

To understand the simple chart we call the point where the personal scent of the handler is gone, and only the track scent remains "THE HUMP". The chart shows you the three main indicators as to when to expect the "HUMP" to take place. This chart is not my idea, it was developed in Europe many years ago and promoted by one of the best trainers of tracking dogs that I knew in Canada, I first met him in the UK, then again later in my second life in Canada.

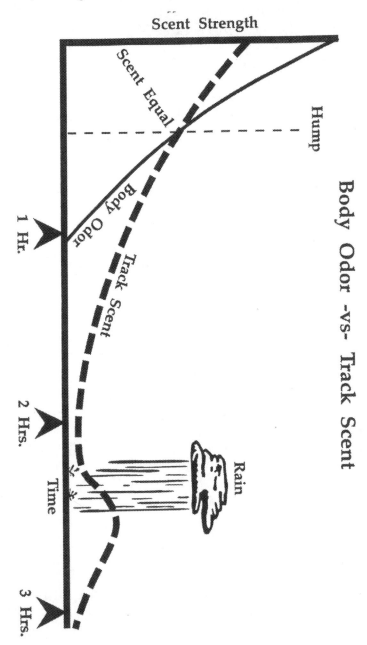

Condition Value Chart for "Hump" Estimation Time

Example #1

Value	3	2	1	Total
Wind	Low	Medium	High	2
Temp	Low	Medium	High	2
Humidity	High	Medium	Low	3
Vegetation	Lush	Medium	Sparse	3
Weather	Overcast	Dull Sun	Bright Sun	3
Time of Day	Morning	Evening	Afternoon	3
			Total	14

14 x 5 min = 70 min to hump (+ - 15%)

Value	3	2	1	Total
Wind	Low	Medium	High	
Temp	Low	Medium	High	
Humidity	High	Medium	Low	
Vegetation	Lush	Medium	Sparse	
Weather	Overcast	Dull Sun	Bright Sun	
Time of Day	Morning	Evening	Afternoon	
			Total	

As part of my education, Wilf insisted that it was time for me to do some judging. His attitude was the more you see the more you learn from other people; and their dogs.

In the UK the system for selecting judges is simple; the club who holds the trial sends the judge's name to the Kennel Club. If there is no reason why he should not judge, the KC upholds the local clubs request. If the novice judge does a good job he will be asked by other clubs, if does not perform well enough, he will not get any more offers. The principle is clear, simple and without the bureaucratic, organized exams on paper, the oral exams, the apprenticeship in dozens of trials under a "licensed" judge, then you can pay a CKC fee and may judge. The obvious fact is that the clubs and competitors approve the judges on the basis of their skill in fair judging. I was happy to judge my first tracking tests, Wilf judged the obedience and other work. It had to happen to me, but it did turn out alright in the end. One of my track layers was carrying a hammer, with which he knocked the start post into the ground. He laid the track in the pattern I had given him then, unbeknown to me, the track layer saw a rabbit in the edge of the field, and he threw the hammer out into the field.

If only he had just continued to lay the track, but oh no, he went and recovered the hammer, then finished laying the track. Yes, you guessed it, a dog started the track very well, and then went over to the hedge to sniff, he did come back and completed the track. I had no idea why the dog left the track, the owner had no reason either. Then my track layer admitted his little trip to get the hammer. No harm done, the dog qualified and the errant track layer had to pay for a few drinks at the pub that evening. Strange things happen at strange times. There was so much fun with the dog people, we all worked hard and in many situations also played hard. Most of the incidents were very small, but to those concerned it was a good laugh.

Very often my fellow club members and I would be at dog trials together, travel together, compete against each other, and then celebrate together.

At one south London show, the conformation exhibitors drew my friend and I to the ring side, not to watch the dogs, but the owners. We made little side bets regarding the "fashions" worn. Which owner with the shortest mini skirt would or should win her class. On a more dangerous note, the money went on the possibility of an overflowing disaster happening with one of the low cut blouses when the owner ran or bent over the dog. Only once did I see it happen, but I lost my bet that day.

One of the big exhibition halls that were used for dog shows always had a slippery floor as it had been used for dancing the night before. Alan, my friend, who also showed and worked his German shepherds, did not like the slip and slide when we ran the dogs. One day we arrived very early at this hall, sure enough the floor was like glass. Alan grabbed two fire buckets full of water and "accidentally" spilt them over the area. We rushed on to the mess with brushes and some mops appeared, soon a lot of people were helping to "dry" the floor. It was nice to work on that day!

No one ever put rubber mats all over the show rings in Europe, the rule was simple; the dog should work on what ever the surface is. This could be difficult in hot hot weather if the surface was asphalt, we used to rub the dogs feet with margarine to stop the tar sticking. It was not good. If the work was outside, it could be lawn cut or six inch grass, even pebbles or gravel. No one got up set; they just got on and worked.

The whole dog scene was a sport and to be enjoyed to the full. Talking of dress and fashions in the rings; no one was ever expected to get dressed up like a fashion plate to show a dog. Casual and clean was the accepted norm. Later after I crossed the pond, I was called to one side by a very smart lady in a most becoming wardrobe; she proceeded to lecture me on dress in the ring. For my shame I had removed my suit jacket and ran around the ring in shirt sleeves and a tie. I was firmly told "Decorum must be retained at all times when in the ring", (Whoops).

Another problem that we did not have in Europe in the 50's and 60's was the professional paid handlers. People if they were fit showed their own dogs and enjoyed it. The financial rewards were not great, but this was a sport. There were a few "Pot Hunters" but not many. Some people did the little things to help their dog. The odd clip here and there, the splodge of talcum powder to whiten up the dog's coat, even a touch of mascara to blacken a pink nose, nothing serious, and I do not think these tricks ever fooled a good judge anyway.

With just over a year to go before being pensioned out of the army, I still had the idea that security dogs might be my future work, so I took on as many part time jobs as possible.

There was a strange one that comes to mind; a clothing and bedding manufacturer asked me to do a job for him. There had been so many break-ins at his factory; no one knew how they got in or why they did so much damage. The factory was a nice modern plant, built on the open space plan and must have been nice to work in.

I was shown a pile of coats and costumes that had been slashed and had oil poured all over them, damage was also done to the machines. It made me a little angry to see the result of such senseless vandalism. I agreed to try to catch the idiots that had made this stupid waste.

I made a deal with the owner, if I caught the vandals in the act, he would pay me five hundred pounds, a huge sum at that time, but much less than he was loosing each time the vandals got in. The other part of the deal was I would work and watch for two weeks. If I had not done the job, I would get nothing. It was a gamble, if successful a little cash for my savings. At night I switched all the inside lights on, and then made my watch point beside the main power switch. I turned them all off and just sat and waited in the dark.

Jinx laid beside me; my plan was that he would hear them before I did, if so I would keep him very quiet until the intruders were well inside. I was in that position for three nights, I was getting worried and thinking I had done the wrong deal. On the fourth night we waited, dozed off or whatever.

After midnight Jinx woke me up, I kept him quiet beside me until I could hear someone moving in the middle of the floor. Then I pulled the main switch. The whole place was flooded with light. When I stood up, I could not believe my eyes, standing in the middle of the floor was a man about 40 years old, he was absolutely naked as the day he was born. In his hands he had an oil can and a large saw, he still was squirting oil over a rack of dresses. I stopped Jinx before he reached the man. He just stood there laughing at me; suddenly he sat down on the floor and burst out crying like a baby. I was just not sure what to do, I told him to give me the saw and the can and he just passed them to me. I got him on his feet and into the office, put a blanket around him and called the police. I was trying to explain that the man was naked, crying and definitely not drunk. They came quickly, called a doctor who arrived, wrapped the man and took him to the hospital. It was quite a night, one I will not forget in a hurry.

Later I was told the full story. The man was the imbecile son of the woman who lived next door to the factory. At night his mother would take his clothing away from him, and lock him in his bedroom or he would wander out into the town. He was smart in a way, he would climb out of his window and crawl over to the factory and get in that way. Eventually he was taken to a mental hospital for help. I felt sorry for him and understood his mothers misguided actions. I do not want another incident like that.

There are "fun" obedience matches European style and "fun" matches North American style. Both are very different in working; by their attitude and organization. In UK a fun match is a club event, and the whole club turns out to see the competition.

The set up is simple; a club will challenge another club to a match. Each match consists of an event at each club. At home and away event is the best way to explain it. Each club will choose a number of dogs in different classes to make up their team.

For example:

> Two test "C" dogs (or UD in NA)
> Two test "B" dogs (open in NA)
> Four novice dogs (nov in NA)

To form a team of eight dogs.

A neutral judge is chosen and on one evening the dogs work the tests alternately. The total score is recorded. The following week at the other clubs venue the same dogs compete again the total scores give the winners of the match.

The club member's support at these matches is amazing. The support for the club's team is to say the least, encouraging. The home club always provides excellent refreshments and all the members mix together and enjoy the evenings. On the other hand the idea of a "fun" match in North America seems to be, either a method of raising funds, or a copy cat formal practice for trials. Anyone who turns up can enter at a fee, you do your class routine and that's that. Sometimes not even a ribbon for top places is offered. It is not a get together of the club members to have fun and support the teams.

I really wish this idea would catch on in North America as it gives all members the opportunity to watch, learn and really get involved in the club. Great pride is felt when your club wins the match.

A little injection of fun. ???

I was having a wonderful time in the 1960's, not much to worry about with my military duties, they all knew I was soon to retire, so left me alone, it was great to go to the obedience trials and the weekends at the working trials. Add to that I was now instructing at two local clubs. Suddenly out of the blue came an invitation from the "British Alsatian Association" to attend their annual instructors' course. As this was only offered to twenty handlers each year, I was very happy.

It did mean a lot of upsets with my routines, both family and competition, but it was a once only opportunity so I took it. Each week end for months I attended classes, both with my own dog and with other people with their dogs. The routine was tough; teach a class a subject, and then the BAA instructors would tear me apart, weekend after weekend.

By the time the final test weekend came round, there were only seven students left out of the original twenty, some quit, some were let go.

On the week end of the final exams we were told to teach various subjects to a class of various standards. For example, I had to teach the "about turn" to a beginner class; then teach scent discrimination to a very advanced group. All that with four examiners watching, listening and writing miles of notes as we worked. The students were great; some of them had been briefed to act stupid or put collars on the wrong way. The strangest thing they set up for me was for one student to come into the class and started to do heel work with his dog on the right side. Thankfully I spotted it as soon as we stepped off. It was hard, it was so thorough and demanding that I despaired of being able to graduate.

At the end of the day, a really good sit down meal was set up for us and all the students from the clubs that had played the part for our teaching.

Frank Reigo, Chair of BAA read the results. My God, I passed. We were given a REAL parchment certificate as that now we could teach all standards at any BAA club. It had been a tough few months, but now it was all worth it to be recognized by your peers.

News soon got around, and I was invited to "guest" at many clubs. With the invitations to judge at obedience trials, I was kept busy.

Time was creeping up on me; after over more than twenty years in the army, I only had a few months to my pension. On top of that "Jinx" was getting older and I virtually had to retire him from competition work, now he was my partner in retirement.

For me it was not retirement but a new way of life. I did hope it would be with the dogs, but that was not very likely. What to do next? Prior to my final day in the army I had two months leave due to me. I spent much of it at Wilf's place. I did need the peace and quiet to make a decision. Family life was not good, in fact there was a divorce and my Ex re-married soon after. The children were taken care of. I won't go into that.

Near Wilf's place was a huge common and pond area, I knew it well as we had used it many times as a parachute drop training zone, the secret was not to land in the pond. AS a common land, many people use to walk and use it for recreation.

One day Wilf and I were just walking our dogs on the common when we saw a mob of people all searching the grass and the bushes. I asked one of them, is a child lost? On no, he replied, it is a valuable wrist watch; there is a reward of 500 pounds for whoever finds it.

We looked at the searchers, Wilf said "no way" and we both went to the pub for a lunch and a beer. There we heard the full story. There was a shooting party out on the common the day before, a "posh" party with shotguns and retriever dogs, plus a champagne lunch in a tent. One member of the party was Princess Margaret, and it was her wrist watch that the hordes were looking for. The bar man said, are you going to get your dogs to search, he knew us and the dogs? "What in that mob, no way!" We enjoyed our lunch. Suddenly the rain came, it poured down and all the searchers came into our pub and we left.

As we were walking home, Jinx found a 12 bore cartridge case, it still smelt of powder, Wilf said, well this is where they were shooting from, let the dogs cast the area so Rolfe, Wilf's dog, and Jinx were set up to quarter down wind, not much hope, Wilf said, but give them a bit of work to do. It happened, Rolfe, gave a bark and came out to Wilf; hanging out of his mouth was the watch. A ten million to one lucky shot. Wilf took it to the police station and left his name, a few days later an insurance agent came and filled out forms. Later the cheque arrived.

From that day on, if anything was lost on the fields, glasses, wallets, or keys, let the dogs have a go first, before humans tramp all over the place.

Wilf used to grind it into me, watch your dog, learn something from him every day, you will never stop learning. He was so right. My last day as a soldier was December 31st; on January 2nd I was sworn in as a police officer and sent to the police school for three months.

I had made the decision now it would be a different life.

Imagine me "A Bobby"?

A "COPPERS LIFE"

There I was, back in a barrack room with ten other men, all recruits for the police force, my mind went back to my first day in an army barrack, noise, shouting and rushing around. Not this time, it was clean, comfortable and quiet. We went to a tailor to be fitted for uniforms, and collected a few strange articles, wooden baton, pair of handcuffs and piles of text books. It was all very civilized.

We were welcomed by the Chief Instructor who told that if this group was normal, half of us would fail, the first negative words we heard. We would be doing physical training at 7 am, breakfast, then classrooms all morning learning what we could do and what we could not do.

First Aid class, unarmed self defense, traffic regulations and a driving test plus evening class after supper; to top this activity, there would be a test every week, fail this and away you go.

We ran and jumped, studied and made notes, we pushed each other around then put broken bones in bandages and splints, it was a very concentrated course. The written exams were hell. The physical instructors threw us around like paper dolls, and the St.

John's examiner was never fully satisfied with our bandages. We had to learn so much off by heart, I can still give a caution to a person arrested and let him or her know that they had a right to a lawyer, all off the tip of my tongue today, forty years later. We practiced with each other, even made tape recordings so we would not make mistakes on exam day. Our teachers and instructors were so good and thorough that we could not help but learn. Oh, we did get the odd week end off.

Finals came so quickly, three days of written work and practical tests. The last day was dreaded. We were all packed up ready to go home. The Chief called us in to his office one by one to give us the good or bad news. Pass or fail. He also told us where we were going to be posted. I must have scraped through, I was lucky, my station would be in Chatham, and there was a police house for me. I would have to sort that out later as I was on my own now.

At my new station I was soon put to work, night duty of course, as all new men were kept in the dark away from civilians for a while. Then the grind began, shift work. 2pm to 10pm. 10pm to 6am. 6am to 2 pm, with shift changes every two weeks. For example, on the 10pm to 6am shift, we ate breakfast at midnight. Quite a change for the body clock, and takes time getting used to. I never did.

My main patrol area was in the Royal Naval Dock Yard; my beat was the area around the nuclear submarine refitting base. Just to add a little excitement to the job, we were required to be armed with a 9mm pistol, this is because the area was considered to be a possible target for the IRA as there had been incidents else where in London and Birmingham. Of course I was one of the older men; there were young men who had joined the force straight out of high school, hence the nick name, "Uncle Art". All in all a good bunch of men, the training school had sorted a lot of people out, so it made sense that the people you work with had a good attitude and manner.

To break the boredom there were a few outside jobs. In those days the workers were paid in cash, so once a week a group of us, in two land rovers, had to go into town to pick up the pay roll; it was a big one as there were 5,000 employees to be paid.

On a few occasions we were sent out on a search warrant to an employee's house who was suspected of stealing tools or even smuggling tobacco and cigarettes from the ships that docked in the port. Apart from that it was just patrol and direct people around the place. Oh and don't forget "If you want to know the time or the nearest toilet", just ask a policeman. It happens all the time.

What about the dogs? I am coming to that.

There was a male black retriever at the station; to say he was a police dog would be putting police dogs in the category of canine comedians. This animal was just a huge pet and he had some very definite ideas as to how he should work on patrol at night. This I discovered when told to do a patrol of my beat with the dog. I should have known better as everyone and anyone used to hook him up and take him on patrol, or as he considered it as "walkies". So it came to pass one dark and dirty night that I picked him up from his kennel and proceeded to patrol my beat and protect the Queens property and keep the peace.

He tugged all over the place ad deposited piles of mud all over my nice clean uniform and my shiny boots. In a very erratic manner we carried on to wander around in the dark. Suddenly the dog stopped, he would not move one inch. My heart was in my mouth, had this idiot of a dog spotted an intruder? Was it a wild Irish boy? I shone my flashlight in the direction the dog was indicating and before me I saw a huge chocolate machine staring back at me. The dog then leapt onto it with glee, barking and making it very obvious that he knew what it contained. I gave in to him, poor thing he must be hungry, I dug into my pocket for a coin and out came a bar of fruit and nut. He devoured the bar faster than it had come out of the machine. We went on our way again, twenty minutes later he stopped again. What now I thought, another machine, no, this time it was a men's washroom door. Like a hero, I flung the door open; the dog passed me like a flash, put his paw up on the wash basin and demanded that I turn on the water. It must have helped to wash the chocolate bar down. For the rest of my patrol this dog refused to pass any vending machine or washroom door.

A. Newman

I admit I was getting pissed off with this performance. This state of affairs had to stop, right here and now. After a little training, corrections, plus a few words of wisdom as to what would happen if he halted at another "comfort stop", and the dog started to fall in line. At 2am I went for a meal break, the other constables were very quiet until one asked how the dog patrol went. Then I knew what the score was. I went back out on patrol and spent all the time working the dog by machines and washrooms. At six o'clock, I went into meal room at the end of my shift. I asked the guys to give the dog some chocolate; the dog took one look at me and refused. I told the guys, it was so nice to have such a well mannered dog to take on patrol.

To the average person this incident would only cause amusement; it did to all the other officers, it was funny at the time. Afterwards I began to think, how was this dog going to detect any intruders? How as this dog going to protect his handler? The answer was simple; he would not and could not. I asked then why was he there? Now here is where I made another stupid mistake, one of many. I mentioned my thoughts to a sub-inspector; he was the last person I should have approached. He told me that I was just a new constable and to mind my own business and not interfere with things that do not concern me or things I knew nothing about.

I should have known better, this person was well know as what we call a "creeper", he crawled around anyone of status high than his; attending the Royal Navy officers mess instead of being a member of the police club. His attitude to those of a lesser rank was arrogant to extreme.

I decided to write a short précis on dogs in police service in a situation like ours; nothing very exciting, just a few notes. The police dog should only have one handler. Both dog and handler should attend the police dog training school. During service the training should be continued to keep the dog alert; just a few obvious observations. I gave it to the shift inspector, who liked it and passed it to the Chief's office.

I was thanked in a letter and told that some changes would be made regarding the use of dogs. Very nice, except the letter was seen by the snot sub-inspector, who accused me of going over his head and I

48

had no right to do anything without his permission. He was so upset at being left out of the dog matter; he then began to give me a hard time. This mismanager of men decided to give me all the dirty jobs and duties, such as car park attendant, and cloak room attendant at functions. He detailed me to everything except picking up paper and dog ends in the street.

I did have the last laugh; I was paired with a Customs officer on watch for smugglers. The dear sub-inspector was just walking out of the gate, when I called his companion for a search. I found a few packets of duty free cigarettes in his coat pocket. The Customs officer seized them and charged the sub's friend with smuggling. I thought it was fair one. A few days later I received a cheque for two shillings, it was a customs reward for the tobacco seized. I never did change the cheque; it brings back so many memories. Keeping inside the rules and regulations, the clown still gave me all the crap jobs, and continually found things wrong with my work. My police federation wanted me to make a formal complaint, but what good could or would it do. Before my two years probation was up I quit. So the decision was made, what to do now?

Involvement with dogs had always been in my mind. In Europe there were not many professional dog schools, due to the proliferation of dog clubs. These clubs were everywhere and provided training, competition and most of all social friendship and sportsmanship. It was a classless sport, everyman and his dog was welcome and could afford the small class fees.

I remembered my trip to Canada where the situation was slightly different. Most groups were set up on a professional basis, or at least a profit enterprise. On the spot decision, I took a trip to Canada to find out the opportunities. Friends there helped me and encouraged me to come and settle in Canada.

On return I applied for immigration and soon had a medical and a long interview with authorities at Canada house in London. I spoke a little French, which did help; I had funds to set up a small business and most of all friends that would sponsor me. It was just a matter of waiting as the wheels turned.

In the mean time a friend who had retired from the police dog school to join the security company of Securicor, offered me a job as long as I was in England.

Wow, this was something new, patrols in a van with my own dog, not Jinx, as he had been retired and my daughter had taken him over. This was my Rottweiler "Dera". To be collecting and distributing bags of large amounts of cash from stores to banks was risky, but with Dera beside me I felt secure.

Fortunately most of the duties were in the day time which left me time to continue to instruct the dog classes at "Medway Towns Club" and the club in "Whitstable" three evenings a week. The classes were big and very demanding, but it was fun always. I also learnt a lot from the other instructors, "Charley Wyant" and "Bing Bellamy", both top competitors and judges.

I travelled with a lady who had two excellent "Shelties" who were good working dogs, no signs of the shy shelties seen in the ring with conformation only, there were exceptions of course, but not many.

It was tough waiting for the permission to fly to Canada, but all you can do is wait. I enjoyed the fairly informal duties with "Securicor"; the other men all seemed to have a sense of humor, especially at tea breaks.

One day the "Boss" called me to the main office, he said, "bring that bloody great dog with you and a flask and sandwiches", you will be here all night. I had no idea what I was in for. When I arrived it was explained that all the electric power had gone off. This did include the huge vault where millions of pounds were kept over night ready for distribution to the big factories as payroll, very few were paid by cheques in those days. The electric locks on the vault were gone as well as all the steel access gate locks and the alarm system. This would all take a few days to fix.

Your job, the boss told me, was to stay in the vault in front of the doors pad, lock the gates behind me and let no one in. He gave me a handgun and said do not use it unless there is a break in. I found a camp bed; put it in front of the vault and that was that. I laid down with Dera beside me for the night.

When patrol came to check on me, Dera would let them know we were both OK.

In the morning the electricians came to fix the problems, I asked my boss, just how much cash was in the vault? He said over four million pounds.

I told him it was a pitty that I did not have my ticket to Canada in my pocket; a few of those bank notes would have set me up with my school. He was good; I received double double overtime pay.

My immigration permit arrived, now I had to move. There was also a problem, my daughter decided to stay with her mother, but my young son did not want to.

This is where fate took a hand. The lady with the shelties said she would look after "Mike" until things were sorted out, so he went happily to live with her.

I bought my one way ticket and sent off two trunks by sea mail. Then the farewells, parties and times I really can not remember too well.

At London Heathrow on a flight with Air Canada to Montreal; this was it. Dera was back at the breeder. I could not take her.

In the air, wondering what I had done, would it be successful? I landed at Gander, through customs and immigration. Now I was a legal landed immigrant; on to Montreal where I was met by friends who were giving me a home until I settled down. Now what?

British Working Trials. Over and back on command.
No problem to a working dog.

Lt. col. Jim Murphy in Egypt with a local dog he trained.

Art with Dena and Rocky, Demo Team at the
Medway Dog Training Club in England.

The Ottawa Junior Kennel Club Drill Team.
Demonstrated at the CKC Certennial.

Kaiser of Mallam Group Win.
#1 in Canada that year. Lots of Fun!

Club Member shows the shirt at the Great Wall of China.

"Storm" developing a nice safe landing technique.

Frost&Wood
SIBERIANS

Full team of Sibes, also all obedience and agility works.

"Waiting our turn to work with the CKC."

OBEDIENCE TRACKING AGILITY

What can I say after 30 years of discrimination by the CKC!
"R dogs" But not all dogs.

K9 KUP 2004 CHAMPIONS

CHAPTER TWO

CANADA, A NEW LIFE

I had left "Heathrow" airport and was sitting in the aircraft just thinking, what had I done? Was this a mistake, how would I end up?

A new country, a new life, would it all work out for the good. Too late to worry now, I had jumped in with both feet, there was no going back.

We landed at "Gander" for customs and immigration, the officer stamped my "Landed Immigrant" paper, he said welcome to Canada, "work hard and you will do well". He turned out to be right, first to Montreal and then the flight continued on to Ottawa. There I was met by my sponsors, a lady and gentleman who bred Rottweilers, in fact she had imported on of my puppies.

When we arrived at their home, I was fed and watered then the big surprise was sprung on me. Pat told me that they were giving me a little house on their property just outside of Ottawa near the little village of Manotick. The shock was not over, she then said "Have we got the dog for you". Out came this beautiful female Rottweiler.

She then told me the history of the dog. Previously owned by a couple, the man was a pilot for Air Canada, the lady was also with Air Canada as a flight attendant. They could not spend much time with Dena, so she had become quite a handful with other dogs as

58

well as a cat killer. Pat said, you will be alone now and Dena needs your guidance as much as you need her as a companion. I know you will sort out her problems.

So that was that, I had a place to live and obviously a bit of a challenge with the dog. On my first day in Canada I realized how lucky I was, due to the kindness, and thoughtfulness of my friends. I had planned on a month to get settled, to get used to the area and figure out the possibilities of starting a new dog training business.

The first job was for Dena to come to an understanding with me regarding her future behavior to all and sundry.

I bought a small pick up truck, you must have wheels here the nearest village was four miles away, and I would need transport when I started work, for work I must.

I soon lined up two jobs, one to drive kids to and from school in a huge yellow bus. The other was to do night work as a security guard. In between, Dena was put through her paces. She did try it on with me, once, and then she found out what it meant to come to an understanding with me. For the rest of her wonderful life she was a dream of a dog. We became partners and had no more problems, dog or cat. There was a little event later on with Dena, I thought it was funny, but I have a twisted sense of humor. We were attending a get together of the Rottweiler Club of Canada. I had sat Dena in a chair beside me, put a hat and a pair of sun glasses on her; she looked a real clown.

The previous lady owner of Dena came along to talk to me, she laughed at the dog and asked if it was one of "Pats" breeding. I told her yes it really is. In fact, it is your Dena!! She jumped back in surprise. Dena did not move; I was so proud other. That weekend we entered three obedience trials, Dena managed to qualify at each trial, thus the title of CD, or companion dog was granted by the CKC.

The club members were happy as there were so few "Rotts" in shows at that time (1971). It was a good boost for the breed. It did not do my reputation any harm as well. Good for my future projects. I hoped!

I could not afford the entry fee at any more trials, or the time and expense of travel and hotels, so the continuation training of Dena became tracking and retrieving. We had a ball; it was so rewarding to work with such a responsive dog. A few obedience people started to drop by my little place, we talked and the subject came round to the tracking. They wanted to find out if their dogs could track. I told them, every dog could track; they do it most of the time they are out of their house. Their nose tells them who has been there and what they did. They follow various trails and their natural instinct gives them information that no human will ever know.

It did seem to come naturally, no school bus on weekend, no security either as they employed part time people Saturday and Sunday.

So our little tracking group started to work; the beginning of my dream of a dog training school. Most of the dogs worked well once they got the idea to follow a "set" scent, most of the people did well. The big problem was the handlers that knew better than the dog and kept pulling the dog off the track. What could I tell the owner, when you can get on your knees and sniff out the track scent as well as your dog, then and only then can you be pushy and aggressive in you handling.

The golden rule "trust your dog" if he fails to work the track it is usually the humans fault in laying and not knowing where you laid. Handlers get lost, dogs rarely do!! Later in the year a few of the dogs took the tracking test and did well.

Next huge event for me came all of a sudden without warning. My sponsors, who owned the property, were divorcing. Before I had time to panic, I was offered the whole patch of land, 25 acres, for a tiny price for its value. I had saved, but not enough to buy, especially as the husband gave me THREE days to raise the cash. The bank was very helpful, and when one of my dog friends offered a $10,000 note to support me, I managed to get the mortgage in time. We went to the Land Registry office and the property was transferred into my name and that was it. I had the land and a house; also on the property was a large building with hydro, water and a toilet; dirty but in good condition.

This was the start of the "All Dogs Sports Club".

My dream was coming true. I remembered the immigration officials in London when I applied to immigrate, they said "Canada is the land of opportunity IF you are prepared to work hard and grab it with both hands", they were right.

Many friends helped me to clean and paint the training Hall. Now I could have classes in winter as well I gave up the night security job. Now it was the training or bust. At first basic obedience training, then as the dogs and students improved and entered trials with good results, we moved up to more advanced exercises and competition work.

From teaching days in England I was always convinced that happy students and happy dogs was the aim. I loved all the dogs of course, and treated the students as personal friends, not just fee paying people. We had and will continue to have, happy classes with fun; treating everyone as part of the club not just customers.

After class we often all went out to McDonalds or Tim Horton's for a coffee and laugh and chat. They were wonderful people. As things settled down I could enter a few trials with my dogs. First, at one time the CKC knew that BORDER Collies were dogs; they were allowed to compete in obedience and tracking trials.

Then the CKC Board made a disastrous decision, BC's were not to be recognized as a breed. Not even for working events. Now BC's were out of the "official" sports.

It is not a coincidence that since that board decision, the working events entries have dropped to an all time low in the CKC trials; where as it was normal to see 20 or 30 dogs per class at the trials. Today (2008) it is more often to have 5 or 6 in classes. Only in top class "Utility Dog" do we see decent numbers, more about cause and effect in part III suffice to say, their aim is to garner points in the repetition of the same old exercises.

The removal of the Border collie was not the only "strange edict" of the board of the CKC. The reasons are obvious, very very few of the board members over the past thirty years have had any experience in training for obedience or tracking, their attitude and decisions prove it every time the board meets.

I have attended meetings of the CKC board all over Canada at my own time and expense. Calgary, Montreal, Toronto, Ottawa. I see it, I hear the attitudes. Conformation rules the board at the expense of the development of the working dogs ability and progress to World Standards. Even at the nice cocktail parties and official dinners, if working sports are brought up in conversation, it is immediately pushed aside, with attitude; I do not wish to know. WHY? Because in general the boards never have understood the working dogs abilities. Not surprising really. If you have not walked the walk, you cannot talk the talk. I will leave it there for the moment.

I and so many like me have enjoyed the training of our dogs. Whether it is for obedience and tracking, lure coursing or den trials; Retriever trials or Agility, the variety of abilities of the dog is endless. There is always room for improvement and progress if we go about it the right way.

Enough maudlin misery, there is so much fun with dogs that overall it takes first place in enjoyment. There are so many incidents that initially seem to be disasters but as "BLOOPERS" give fun for years after they occur.

Even after 25 or 30 years someone will refer to my "Double send away" in a utility class, this one was in Rochester, N.Y. I always took my Border Collies with me when they worked different classes. This time Bonnie was in Open and Mac was in Utility. I went into the ring with Mac; I left Bonnie by her crate. All went well until I set up for directed jumps. Mac was keen to go out, I made sure he was straight then sent him. He was as straight as a die, but!!! So was Bonnie, she had come into the ring and as I sent Mac, she decided to go out with him. I hollered "SIT" and stood their looking at two dogs both waiting for the jump command. I had never felt so small in all my life. I just want to run and hide.

The spectators did not help, they were roaring with laughter. After a few moments it settled down, now what would the Judge say? She was wonderful, I loved that lady. In a very loud voice she said "Nice try Sir but no double points". This and other "Bloopers" lived on long afterwards as a source of fun.

Back at the homestead, life went on, teaching, working my dogs and the constant maintenance of buildings and kennels. By now I had nice fenced rings on my fields, lots of grass to cut. One day a dear friend came around, what are you doing this evening? Never mind you are coming out with me to see something interesting. That's all she would tell me. I knew that "Thea" would not say much as she drove me out to a house a few miles away. I saw about twenty people, all with German shepherd dogs all over a large field, I did not know just what they were really doing. "Come on" said Thea and took me to a tall older man and introduced me.

In a very positive and forthright tone he told us that he had decided to teach German shepherd owner the "New" sport of Schutzhund (ScH). Thea pulled me away and said "Just come and watch and keep quiet".

The gentleman then got all the dogs in a row in front of him, told the owners to "Hang on to the dogs". He then ran up and down the line of dogs shouting, waving a big stick and a plastic garbage bag in the other hand. The dog's reactions were obvious. Some barked and pulled on the leash, some hid behind their owners, the rest just stood there wondering what the hell was going on; so did I. He then explained that he had "agitated" the dogs to see if they had the courage and drive to be a real Schutzhund dog!!!

I looked at Thea; she just burst out laughing at my face. I did manage to say "What the hell is going on here, who is that guy?" "I knew you would love this" she said, that's why I gave you no warning. I replied "thanks for nothing, can we go home now?"

Later it was explained that the gentleman had seen a group in Toronto practicing ScH, he thought it was good for German shepherds. So he rushed in, with very little research to teach the sport. A few weeks later he told the students that he was "not" going to continue training. No reason, just finish.

Thea brought a few of the people to my place. She asked me to explain the sport and just what was required for ScH. They were really nice people so I showed a small film and with Dena did a short track, then the jumps and retrieve. The main point I tried to get over to them was that it is a SPORT, not a bunch of uncontrolled animals biting and attacking humans on "hate" principle. So Sunday mornings started, at 7 a.m. All dogs worked at the tracking, afterwards the obedience routines. Absolute voice control was demanded.

We started with 16 dogs and handlers. At the end of the first six training sessions we had a serious meeting. It was obvious that some dogs and some handlers were not suitable for this sport.

Reasons were various, the attitude of the handler, i.e. just wanted to have a "guard" dog. The dogs, one obviously had hip dysplasia, a couple of the dogs were very shy with weak temperaments. We all discussed the various problems In a good friendly way.

The result was that seven dogs would continue training for ScH. The others would work on the CKC obedience system.

Now we had a small group of suitable dogs to progress on to the basic "Protection" work. To keep it short, we progressed to a good standard. After 18 months of solid hard work, I registered the group as "the Upper Canada Schutzhund Club". Of course we had to register with the German "DVG" or "Working Dog Club". The CKC had no idea of the ScH, and does not today.

We held our first trial with a judge sent over from Germany. He also gave a day clinic for all of us. Some dogs passed, some did not make the grade, but we all learnt so much over the three days.

The following year at our second trial all the dogs did very well, we also had some excellent dogs come to work from the USA and Quebec, over 45 entries. The German Judge gave us some compliments and it all seemed to be worth the years of hard work and efforts by the handlers of the wonderful dogs.

The ScH group continued to train and work together, my input was less and less, I had the obedience classes as well as the kennels to take care of. Eventually the group purchased a small piece of land and moved away, they planned to build a new club house. I wished them well for the future.

My dream was doing well, over the years it had built up and students were achieving success in the obedience rings. It is the student's progress that counts, we were all friends and supported each other when winning and blowing the tests. We travelled together and after the trials were over we went for a meal together.

Winning ribbons is always great but the enjoyment of the dogs, the friendships are much more important.

THE "FAR" SIDE

The vast majority of competitors in every sport and recreation are great people; they accept the ups and downs of the game! When they fail one attempt, you hear them say, never mind, we will do better next time. There is always the next time to look forward to.

However, there is a very tiny element that does not have this sportsman like attitude. Few, very few, thank goodness revert to cheating in one form or another. How can this happen you say, the rules are clear, and other spectators are watching as well?

A little story about a competitor from the USA in a trial in Canada; while having a smoke break outside the show arena, I watched a lady sending her Golden Retriever on send aways, time and time again. I realized that the TARGET to which the dog was being sent was a very large yellow water bowl.

I wondered why she did not change direction and send to other spots. I thought, oh well everyone has their own ideas and methods of training. Smoke over, back inside to watch the dogs work. I then noticed the lady had a chair at the end of the utility ring. As she got up to go into the ring to start work, she put the huge yellow dish in front of her chair. I continued to watch it was a nice working dog and did very well. Then came the send away for directed jumping; sure enough the dog shot across the ring and on the ladies command turned and sat, almost on top of the yellow bowl. The team completed the class and did very well. After she left the ring she put the water dish, without water, into a bag.

I realized she was just using the dish as a target. What should I do? Mention it to a steward, even approach the lady. Maybe mind my own business. I decided to take another route.

When the afternoon trial started, the lady went through the same routine. When she saw the direction of the send away, she moved her chair to the center by the ring. Sure enough, when she got up to go into the ring, she placed the yellow target there again. This proved to me that she was cheating.

All I did was go and pick up the dish and move it out of sight behind the spectators.

I watched her face as she set the dog up for send away, no big yellow target!!! She was visibly upset and when the dog was sent, it stopped half way looking around for the dish. She failed, was angry. When she found the dish there was a little note in it. "CHEATS NEVER PROSPER"

I went home happy.

Another example of the attitude of win at all costs, or is it?

I personally knew a young man who had worked long and hard to train his German shepherd to track, it was an excellent tracking dog, BUT, this young man had a big problem. Although the dog was a beautiful example of a shepherd, it had no CKC registration papers, therefore, could not be entered into CKC trials. What on earth could he do to get into the trials?

He did the obvious, which I believe many others have done because of the no "non registerable" rules. He bought another German shepherd, same sex, same age, then took the registration papers and applied them to his wonderful tracking dog. Just to avoid any questions, he gave the new registered dog to some people a long distance away; they had no interest in the tattoo number on the dog's groin. The newly "papered" dog entered many trials; TD and TDX were no problem to the dog.

Now, think, he did break the rules of the CKC. What difference did it make to anyone or any other dog? None, it just put another dog into the sport, the entry fee supported the club promoting the tracking trials, plus the CKC got their cut from the entry fee.

The sole reason why this man broke the rules was to enjoy the sport. He would never have had to go to these extremes if the CKC discrimination rules had not prevented "None registerables" from entering, enjoying the sport, plus putting a few dollars into the clubs.

Was this blatant cheating?

Would you have reported him?   No, I did not on principle.

Here are a few little tricks that some people get up to in efforts to win. OR put it another way, get an advantage over those who do not cheat, just play the game according to the rules of the sport.

While acting as a ring steward at a trial in southern Ontario, I came across another "trick" used by a competitor in utility class. Part of my duties was to place out the scent articles, remove three (in those days) and show the judge the articles.

When I picked up the metal article I noticed that the bar was covered with transparent scotch tape. Obviously this was to prevent the dog from touching the metal, which was the object of the exercise.

I appreciate that some dogs do not like metal in their mouth. If the dog can not retrieve metal articles he fails; simple and clear.

I did draw the judge's attention to the tape on the metal bar. Very quietly the judge spoke to the competitor and he did disqualify the dog.

I knew the handler very well, but for the past 20 years she has not said a word to me, oh well.

Why should she expect to get away with her cheating, when other handlers work so hard to overcome these problems?

Some people are surprised at the tricks people get up to, just to beat others and get a slip of   ribbon.

Hey, there's more!

In the tests of sit and down out of sight of the dog, some handlers worry, we all stand around corners, behind vehicles and "TWITCH". If the dog stays it is a relief.

Some handlers have a novel way of <u>not</u> getting uptight while away from their dogs. It really is simple, look around at the next trial you go to watch.

For example, with gender bias, the wife gives the command stay and is marched off somewhere. But wait a moment, her husband has taken up a good position outside the ring, he is staring at the dog, the dog likewise. Is this fair? Is it really cheating? Or a case of opportunity is there. If this "positioning" happens at every trial, it is cheating.

Another little one.

One handler's dog has done very well in the first part of the trial, but now another dog that has done better at previous trials has entered the ring. One wonders why the first handler is now standing near the ringside bouncing a ball for her Border collie to bark and get excited.

The dog IN the ring is distracted and drops a few points. Question, was the distraction deliberate?

We have to decide if it really is cheating, bad manners or ignorance.

In the remote possibility the reader might be a conformation handler or owner; their rings are not off the hook.

One of the incidents I witnessed was maybe bad manners or frustration OR!!!!

The class was finished flying around the ring, then strutting its stuff; the judge had made her decision. "You first, you second, you third". Out of the ring they came, the owner of the third ribbon goes over to a garbage bin and throws the ribbon in. Clearly stating to all and sundry, "that's all it is worth".

Of course the judge was upset, but fortunately a club steward witnessed the insult to the judge, made a report and the ribbon disposer was fined and suspended for a year. Manners make the good competitor.

I always liked to show my dogs if they were of fair to good conformation standards. So I used to pop into the show ring with my German shepherds and my Rottweilers, <u>not</u> my Border collies, they are "Canine non gratia" in the conformation world, in North America at least. (1975)

So I trundle around at high speeds, show teeth and the dog accepts groping with out complaint.

We dash around again and the Judge delivers the verdict; all good fun. After winning sufficient points to make my "Misty" a Champion, I found out that I was supposed to withdraw from the next two classes that I had entered and paid for. Why? If I stayed in the "Open" class and happened to win some more points, they did not mean anything to my dog. However, if I transferred to the "Specials" class, it would leave the points for the dogs in "Open". My selfish attitude was No. I paid and entered open; I am running   in "Open".

Oh my, the "professional" handlers were so angry with me. I told them, beat my dog and the points are yours, if you cannot beat my dog then what does it prove, if my dog is pulled it just sets free points for you. Good Luck, Beat my dog, I won't mind. After a few threats and a few offers they left me alone. So I thought, until we got in the ring.

First the "pro" behind me pushed his dog's nose up my dogs back end, she did not like that, and I looked at the "pro" he just grinned. SO, I used my grooming brush on Misty, from a line head to tail, whoops the brush accidentally bumped the dog behind on the nose, now she was upset, but the "pro" kept his distance. All well and good until we started to run around the ring; the other "pro" kept cutting me off at the corners. I realized what they were doing between them.

I thought this can be fun next time around. As we came to the top corner I skipped back to put the pro handler inside against the ring fence, he took the bait and went past me. Suddenly he "bumped" into my hip and went flying over the ring fence. At the end of the class the Judge was laughing as he gave me first. He said in a very quiet tone, nice hip check, good as the NHL. He knew what was going on.

The handler spoke to me after saying that was a hell of a class and laughed. We became very good friends after that. In fact, he showed some of my dogs for me when I began to have hip problems.

You never know what is going to happen in the ring.

A couple of "one liners" to break the monotony:

Judge:

Madam, if you are going to blacken your dogs nose try using water proof dye, my fingers are black.

Judge:

You have a beautiful dog sir, but she will not get far in this ring, these are males.

After waiting a long time for a dog to finish peeing, the Judge said "that dog is responsible for the water shortage in this province".

Club Secretary:

No madam, the miscellaneous class is not for dogs of unknown parentage.

Judge in a black suit to white poodle owner:

If I had known you would bring a dog with so much chalk powder, I would have worn a white suit.

Judge to me when I presented my Rottweiler: "Does he Bite" my reply "only when he eats"

NEW CHALLENGES

In the mid 1980's it was becoming obvious that entries were falling in the working sports of the CKC. From good entries of 25 to 30 dogs in each class, they were getting smaller, down to 5 to 10 at trials.

Entries for tracking trials were becoming so low that many clubs with good history of excellent trials, just gave up promoting them and without trials the training almost ceased to be in the clubs programs.

Some reasons were discussed at high levels; however nothing positive was offered to promote the events. Some gave high entry fees as a cause. Some gave boredom and lack of excitement at trial venues. Some said, all day for six minutes (plus stays) for high entry fee was a reason.

Whatever the reason, it was still happening; a few clubs even gave up the tradition of obedience trials after many years.

I can not speak for others, but I decided to stop going to the obedience trials in the late 1980's; my reason, no attempt at all to renew the current tests in any constructive and progressive manner, to make them more exciting and challenging.

Some changes were promoted as milestones in the sport. For example; the following of the AKC rule that required handlers to keep their hands at their sides during all recalls and retrieves. What a monumental decision!! This will bring handlers back to the sport in droves.

Most people understand that the raw beginner and the novice are the foundation of any project. The "Top Brass" does the thinking but the grass roots do the work. It was decided to increase the number of classes that owners could enter.

For the beginner, a pathetic Pre-Novice appeared. The test reflected the standard that any beginner could achieve with approximately five lessons. Oh by the way the entry fee was still high and equal to the now multitude of utility classes. Now for the experienced dogs, not only could they pass three tests, all the same for UD but now pass more and more for points to become an Advanced Champion. Even better, go on and on doing the same tests over and over you can become a Master Champion.

Where are new tests and exercises? None apparently.

My opinions are my thoughts to make the sport more exciting but most of all to challenge the trainers and owners to <u>TEACH</u>, not everlasting <u>repeat</u> the same old routines.

Is it possible for a new set of exercises to be put together? Not variations of the North American system; new tests that have been carried out across the world for years.

First and foremost, I fully understand that in North America ALL classes have to have titles on offer. Without titles where would we be, especially as every one seems to have them? So do not attack me for getting rid of titles, I know it cannot happen. Especially as the CKC now controls the awarding of 27 titles for dogs.

Could a valiant effort be made to look forward to interesting and effective tests and exercises?

First think about progress to the next class, i.e. some preparation for the future. Does the Novice test have any bearing to the open test? Just heel work.

Let's think of a few exercises:

1. Heel work: Object of the work is to progress from on leash to off leash.

    Keep it basically as is.

    OR

    A few advances: Left and Right abouts

    Hold slow pace for ten steps

    Hold fast pace for ten steps.

    Left, right turns in slow & fast pace

    Already improvement.

2. Keep figure of eight, most dogs need it

    Introduce a Retrieve Exercise

3. Dog to retrieve ANY safe object provided by owner.

    (Currently a beginner test world wide)

4. Remove the lease from Stand for examination to prove this umbilical cord is not necessary. (Long gone in the AKC)

5. One minute Sit

6. Two minute down, handlers back's to dog.

7. The Recall: from 20 feet.

    Dog to stop in front of handler.

    Handler to put leash on dog without moving or dog moving.

Finish ON the lease, loose.

This of course requires the handler to have the leash.

The old saying "Handler and Leash should never be parted, with dog on or not."

Leash to be placed around handler's neck "sash" style when ever a dog is worked off lead. NOT on the stewards table.

(The rest of the world does this)

So does this prepare the dog for Open Retrieve? Yes

Advances, Stand, Yes or UD Test

Out of sight, or eye contact, Yes

Not too much of a drastic change. Improved heel work required and cuts out "body" signals in down.

Give 50% points for handler's excessive voice & leash, but permit pass if not unqualified heel work.

NEW ENDEAVOURS

After returning home from a trip to England, I mentioned the fun and enjoyment that the dog people in Europe were having with an organized sport called "Agility" I explained that it had developed from the military and police forces obstacle training routines.

Now it was organized with rules, standards and equipment. The sport was sweeping across Europe. Of course the British Kennel club had recognized the sport and promoted it to all clubs across the nation.

I basically explained the object of the game, to jump various jumps, climb up dog walks and run through tunnels.

My students wanted to try it!!! I build some jumps, a see-saw and dog walk, managed to get a plastic tunnel and we started to play the game. Our dog walk was planks on top of old 40 gallon drums. An old truck tire was rigged to let the dogs jump through. The obstacle that was most difficult for the handlers and their dogs was the "weave"; it also gave us the most laughs and plenty of fun getting the dogs used to weaving in and out. The original people who started to practice our agility also did a lot of work building and painting the equipment. I have to recognize the wonderful people, without their efforts agility would not have started then, Thea Boshart, Marylyn Frazer, Elizabeth Neilsen and M.J. Theot.

After only one year, we had a new full set of equipment, twenty dogs performing; I do mean performing, as we were asked to give demonstrations all over the area. Enquiries came in from all over Canada, especially from out west. As a result we formed a national club.

The Agility Dog Association of Canada, ADAC, that's where it all started. The membership exploded, it was too much for me to manage, so a committee with reps across Canada was formed. To comply with the language law, the new became:

Agility Association Canada (AAC)

I was invited to give clinics at many new formed clubs, the most exciting and rewarding was to go to Vancouver to give a clinic and then to Judge the first trial in the west.

Without getting back to the main theme of this scribbling, I did approach the CKC with a view of the club recognizing and promoting this new sport. Thankfully, as it turned out, I was told "it is just a phase, a flash in the pan; it will never last and will soon fade away".

Today, thousands of AAC members, many AAC clubs, plus many efficient trials all over the nation; formed by the dog people a wonderful success due to dog people. Years later the CKC realized what was happening, people left obedience for the fun and excitement of Agility. The CKC did the obvious, "If you cannot beat them, join them". They did but as usual changed many of the rules at the same time. WHY?

And of course only "Pure bred dogs were allowed"!!!!

The USA was interested in agility at least a year before it came to Canada. Their main association was formed "the Unites States Dog Agility Association" (USDAA). A gentleman, Ken Tashe was the prime mover and did wonders to get agility started in the United States.

I was surprised and pleased to be invited to "Houston, TX" to help with a clinic with two gentlemen from the British Kennel Club. All went well; I even judged one of the trials, and then sat as a time keeper for the other. The venue was the huge hockey arena, each day there were thousands of spectators in the stands, the dogs were shown on TV and the promotion was fantastic.

The following year I was again invited to go to "Dallas" to be part of the examining committee for new Judges. I was pleased to see a Canadian lady as a candidate. P.J. Thout, from Montreal, again pleased that she qualified as a USDAA Judge. Two little side trips that I enjoyed on my "Houston" visit, one to be take to the top of the huge Astro Dome base ball stadium, the other was to be "initiated" as a citizen of Texas; big hat, cowboy scarf and a "genuine" Texas passport. It really was fun there. Getting there, not so much fun, four changes of aircraft! Thank goodness this was before all the "Homeland Security" routines.

Back home, preparing for our first big titles trial; the venue was the "Canadian Guide Dog for the Blind School". Our group supported the school then and we still do today. Weather was fine, many good entries from Toronto, Montreal, some from the USA; a success. Top dog overall was a Shetland sheepdog "Phoenix", not a Border collie, how did that happen?

Phoenix worked nicely and steady all day, I have to admit that many of the Border collies were fast, too fast and too many mistakes; Oh well.

I must write out a hundred times "I MUST NOT BE BIASED" (somehow)

I must admit that throughout the years we have always had excellent relations and co-operation between the Ottawa Border Collie Club and our club. They help at our events, we help at their events, that's how all clubs should get along. Unfortunately that is not the case with most groups. I do not know why, we are all dedicated to Dog Sports and obviously love our dogs others dogs, any dogs.

Agility did progress, three big rings and a puppy training ring on the field, plus the training hall for basic winter work. The theme was always "Fun", even when we designed a local event, mainly for dogs without qualifying agility titles.

We held four events during the summer. Dogs were organized into teams of ten, each team entered the four events but only the four highest scores counted for points.

It was a success, most years we have at least sixteen teams from the area entered.

After the four events of the season, the team with the best scores will win the "K-9" Cup.

The good thing about the K-9 event is that ALL dogs get a chance to run in a competitive way, scores and titles do not really matter as long as the teams have fun together and the dogs gain experience as well as have a good time.

Agility sport has shaken up the dog training sports world, now it really can be fun for both ends of the leash.

THE DARKER SIDE

I think maybe I have painted life full of fun, lots of happy times with the dogs I have come in contact with.

There were the bad incidents that broke my heart and did upset me.

One that stands out in my memory was particularly painful.

Two friends from Southern Ontario arrived with a dog; they asked me to assess the dog in general.

It was a large Golden Retriever, about two years old. I took him for a walk and then up to my training hall. All the time I was with this dog I had a very bad feeling. His attitude and manner was so up tight all the time. His eyes really worried me; I felt that if I relaxed a fraction he would go for me. After an hour I put him back into his crate and went back to the house to talk to the ladies. It was tough; I told them that I would be brutally honest with my opinion of the dog. They said that is just what we came to you for, so give us the decision.

My report was simple and to the point.

I think this dog is a "rogue" dog and can be very dangerous; his attitude, body language, but most of all his eyes. I feel so tense with him; it is as if I expect him to attack me if he either gets the chance or if he just feels like it.

I was surprised at the ladies reactions to this horrible opinion, they agreed, then told me the dog had bitten one of them in the face, attacked another man and hurt him seriously. They asked "What would you do with him?" My reply was simple, you will not like this but to me there is only one thing to be done. He must be put down before he really does serious injury to anyone, including you.

The talked it over then said "We cannot take him to the Vet, will you arrange it for us. It was a Sunday afternoon, but I phoned my Vet and explained the situation, "bring him down now" said Dr. Rabb. The matter was taken care of and a few days later he called to give me the results of an autopsy. The dog's brain was a mass of active cancer. I phoned my friends and told them that he had been a very sick dog and the problem was not of their making.

They were unhappy, I was also but we all knew that the right choice had been made. Now we all go on with new dogs, happy and we pray, fit dogs. Nobody forgets these incidents in a hurry.

We have to remember and accept that it comes to all of us the old senile dog. How do we approach it? If the dog is still fairly happy and has some mobility and bowel control, we love him and nurse him to what we hope will be a natural and peaceful end; however if the situation is putting the dog in pain or in a situation of abject misery, it is only humane and to show our love for him by helping him to end the misery that <u>HE</u> feels.

Even with our own dogs things can go astray. Years ago I was the proud owner of two German shepherd females, individually on their own they were cool calm dogs. They both picked up ribbons and titles at shows and trials; but never let them loose together, it was pure canine hate, they would fly at each other and hurt each other, and they were not playing.

On this particular day, one female was in my study with the door firmly closed, the other was brought in to have her nails trimmed. My partner looked into the study, but did not quite close the door. Next thing I knew, two dogs on top of me attacking and savagely biting each other. L knocked one dog downwards, her teeth managed to go down my leg, ripping as they went. The other dog I managed to grab and throw into the study and slam the door. It was all over in a split second. The results, sixty stitches in my leg from one dog and half an inch of thumb missing from the other. It was a mistake, an accident but goes to show that you must be so careful with problem dogs around. Another incident, I had kennels at one time and used to board dogs. I was careful to find out the habits of my boarders if possible. The dog in question was a sweet dog, not a nasty bone in her body. The owner did tell me that she can climb anything. So I put her in a nice big kennel and run with the mesh right up to the roof. No way could she climb that to get out. Again the human element came into the game. My kennel person was cleaning and washing out the kennels. She put the "Climber" into a run with only six foot fence while she cleaned out. The obvious happened; the dog flew up the mesh, over the top and just took off. Within minutes we were all out searching for the dog. We heard the scream of car brakes. Yes, as quick as that she was on the road and had been killed.

I had to tell the owner, it was so difficult. The cleaner was having a break down, I did not want her hurt any more; so I left out the "run switch" and took the blame. I was sick for the owner; I offered restitution, a pick of any dog. He just said no thanks, she will be hard to replace. He just walked away. I was sorry for the dog. I was sorry for the owner. I was sorry for the cleaner. But I suffered so much for a long time after that. I do not want to dwell on this unhappy side of owning and losing a dog friend, but it is there the wonderful aftermath of these disastrous events is the complete sympathy and support that is given to the loser by all the friends and members of our club and group. Their kindness and understanding helps to overcome the loss.

I say it day in and day out, over and over again, *"dog people are the salt of the earth"*.

SEE THE WORLD WITH A DOG

Traveling all over Canada and quite a piece of the USA has been on the most part a great experience. To meet new dog friends, see new provinces and stat3es as well as visit and stay in so many different towns and cities. Hours and hours of driving might not be so good, but you see new sights all the time.

Of course I have a favorite trip, the three obedience and confirmation shows that used to be promoted by the German Shepherd Club of America. At that time, a few years ago the AKC did not allow three shows in three days at the same venue.

The result, we travelled to trial number one near Buffalo, the club hosting the trial had arranged our rooms in motels on site. Everything went so smoothly, the first trial over, the club checked our room to make sure all was in order then we could check out. If the rooms were dirty, dog hairs in the bath and even worse, we paid a penalty deposit, very fair. Then into the vehicles and off to Syracuse, the next trial. To be in a huge long convoy of dog vans, campers and trucks was quite a sight. All happy, singing and waving. We all just hoped that the leading vehicle knew where he was supposed to be going. He did.

Arrive at the next venue, clean up, meals with the other people, great friendship, then all out to the fields to run the dogs together. Golden rule of course, your dog does it, you pick it up. Everyone did.

A night sleep and on with the show, then back in the dog train and on to Rochester, N.Y.

On the final evening the major awards etc at a nice sit down dinner.

We all said goodbye, see you next year and away back home. To me it was the event of the year for many reasons. The good organization, the friends and also I did very well with the ribbons and the trophies or my dog did.

On the road again, I had been invited to join a "training camp", mainly to explain how the Schutzhund sport worked, but it developed into a tracking clinic. A friend who was also involved in Rottweilers organized a number of instructors of different dog sports to come to North Carolina, Ashville in particular. Each instructor would have set periods during the six days, Monday to Saturday.

I stayed at the beautiful home of my friends parents. Never to be forgotten. This home was right at the top of a mountain in the famous "Smokey Mountain Range". From my home to Ashville was estimated to be at least a sixteen hour drive. Too much for me in one leap, so I stopped off half way in a nice motel, off again in the morning early. Most of the route was on the Interstate highway until I got as far as Johnson City. Then the fun began. I had a little smooth coat black and white Border Collie with me; she was my best tracking dog ever. We drove getting nearer to the mountains all the time. At the bottom of what looked the steep stuff, I stopped off at a little shack that had one solitary gas pump outside it; best to fill up before doing the high stuff.

Meg and I got out stretching our legs etc, an old man came out and I asked him to fill the wagon. In went the hose and he began to crank the pump handle, oh god, how old was that pump?

To pass the time I threw a piece of road gravel for Meg to retrieve, which she did. I kept throwing it onto a pile of gravel. The old man came over, I paid him and she said "does she get the same stone or any one she finds?" I explained she smells my scent on the one I throw and brings that one to me. I could see that the old man was not convinced, so I asked him to mark a stone with his pencil, he did and I handled it for a moment and threw it onto the pile. Quickly Meg brought it back and I gave it to the man. He saw his mark. Then he called back to the little shack. Out came some children and a woman, he told them about Meg and the stone. We had to do it over again for the family.

I told him I was going up the mountain, he said be careful of the lumber trucks, get in the side holes if you hear their horns, they do not slow down. Now I began to worry. Up we started low gear very steady. I passed two black vans with several men in suits and ties; they just watched me go by. Onward and upward, no horns yet, after at least half an hour I came to the house, my friend was there to direct me in. We knew you were on the hill, she said so we were expecting you. I could not figure out how she knew and asked. Don't worry she replied, laughing, we have the bush telegraph, she added, the gas man was impressed with your little dog. Now I was really mixed up. In and rested, Meg fed and spoilt, then relax with a cool beer.

The Rottweilers were all over the place, nice looking and well behaved dogs. Then I learnt something new. Come and look at this she said, and on one of the dogs back was a big black blob, or bubble. What is that? It is a "Tick"; they get on the dogs, bury their heads and feed on blood. To remove them we never pull or the heads stay in and cause sores. She put some fluid on the tick, it curled up and she picked it off and put it into a can with a little gas in the bottom. She explained that this area was bad for ticks, so check Meg often. Every day you learn something.

I remembered the men in suits at the bottom of the mountain, I asked my friends who were they? They laughed and said, they are the Revenue men, government men who are trying to catch the "mountain men" smuggling "white lightening", or liquor off the mountain.

The Hill Billies know and do not get caught very often with the illegal liquor, and then she further said here have a drink. I did and found out why they call it "White Lightening".

We sat on the veranda, the mist over the mountain looked like smoke, hence smoky mountain. I said, am I hearing things, I thought I could hear music. It is the people of the mountain, they play and sing most evenings I was told. I was like going back in time.

So peaceful.

The next morning, bright and early we went in her Volkswagen to Raleigh, the site for the clinic. It was a huge area of empty tobacco barns, nothing in them, it was explained that the tobacco harvest had been lost that year due to weather and bugs. There was a lot of unemployment and poverty in the area.

We met the other instructors and checked equipment for the clinic the next day. I had tracking line and harness for Meg, and also a padded sleeve to show the protection elements of SchH.

Then we went round the shops picked up a few gifts and then learnt another lesson of life. We went in to a grocery store for bits and pieces. The first thing I noticed is that no one paid with money or cash, it was all stamps. I asked why? The manager was with us and he explained that due to the crop failure there was no or little work around. So the government gave out welfare stamps for food and for food only. The workers were having a hard time. I stopped to think, here I was with my dog, both of us eating very well, driving hundreds of miles buying what we wanted. Here people needed help just to feed the family. I felt a little guilty that my life was so good and worry free.

If it had not been for the Dogging experience I would never have know that people in the richest nation in the world were going short of basic food. Back in the house my friend's father and I sat on the veranda with a cool beer. He then asked a strange question. How many young men did you see today? I realized, hardly any, where are they? I was told; young men join the army and send some money to their families. That is all they have to exist on. That is the way of life down here.

The next day the training started. I lectured; Meg worked in our set periods. It was so hot in the barns. We broke at 11 a.m. until 4 p.m. due to the heat. For the tracking we went away from the city to some fields. Every one worked hard each day and did at least have an idea what SchH and tracking was all about.

I expect people will wonder what the economy of North Carolina has to do with dogs. If it was not for the dog sport I would never have travelled so far and so often to other places. Yes lots of fun, but education and understanding of many other people and places occurred.

About time for another "Friendly" dig at the Canadian Kennel Club.

Just a little story of a week in the life of an obedience competitor in the UK. Entry in, off to the trial, oh, did I say entry, that includes the fee for the class I wish to enter. In Canada at the time of this scribble the class fee is at least $25, or thirteen pounds sterling. My fee in the UK is £5 max (five pounds). If I do well in my class there will be a few shillings as well as a ribbon. Nice eh.

On to the trial, I work my dog, the judge makes out the score sheet, normal you say, but the UK judge will also write a short few words or critique on the first four or five dogs, if not more. At the end of the day the judge will put the results into an envelope and post it at once to the Dog Magazine. Official results go to the club officer and without delay sent to the Kennel club, not a month later. Thus even through hell and high water both the KC and the Dog Magazines get the results within a few days, two at the outside.

Now here is the efficiency, the Dog Magazine will pop through my mail box on Friday, if not before with the results. With the current system, clubs have at least 30 days to get the judges sheets (no critiques) to the CKC. For a CKC trial in January we read the results in July or even later.

With the new CKC system, we do not get ANY results in the "Dogs in Canada". We are told it is quicker to put them on to the computer. Want to be on it? Many people do not have a computer!!!

This show and ancient system also works very well with the minutes of Board Meetings. I.e. I have just read the minute of September last year, today is June.

We are told again and again that the CKC is a business. So how many shareholders in any other business will wait for minutes of meetings that are over six months out of I date. In the eyes of the beholder the "Dogs in Canada" is still being powered by two mules, on has a broken leg.

At the very least, the membership deserves a new up to date magazine, at least every month with current information and no late stale news.

Apex has a responsibility to the members. This modern age of computers and printing is the only communication we have. I have always supported the CKC, but for many members like me it is so frustratingly slow and unable to react to today's life style. That's it, now I will shut up for a while.

P.S.

Can anyone give me any reason for any obedience owner to be a member of the CKC?

   i.   We do not register litters of puppies

  ii.   We rarely transfer dogs, we do not sell them

 iii.   We do not get trial results

 iv.   We do not initiate breeding agreements

v.   We do not "vary" breed standards

vi.   We do not introduce "rare or new" breeds

.....SO......

BACK TO FUN AND GAMES

Over the years we have had so much fun with the dogs as a group of friends and owners.

Some of the best times were when we all decided to form a "Drill Team". And what a team it was the first time we started to train. From big Rottweillers to small Tibetan Terriers, with Poodles and German shepherds. The team consisted of twenty dogs and owners. What could be better we thought, than to model the display on the RCMP musical ride, their exercises and patterns were excellent for us to duplicate. For months and months we practiced, getting everyone to know their left foot, and where to go and who to follow. Gradually we put it all to music and it worked. Of course there were collisions and dogs getting lost in the circles and cross overs, these were treated with roars of laughter, then I screamed "do it again". It was worth it for the fun we had. The big day came and we were invited to put on the display at the "Show of Show" in Ottawa. First part was group patterns, the then individual dogs did their thing, finishing up all together. The spectators loved it, we loved it, and I am sure the dogs loved it as well. Later some bright person had the idea to for a "Children's team" from the junior classes we held on Saturday mornings.

Can you imagine my situation, twenty children with all sorts of dogs at various stages of obedience, of even basic control? That was not the biggest problem, the parents; they all tried to chip in with advice while the kids were working on the floor. I really had to lower the boom. I told them, "When they are finished working you can have them back". It worked like a charm.

It took over a year to get the children working as a team, but they became so good. Remember children from seven years to fourteen years of age often have "peer" problems.

The final display was of thirty minutes duration. NO VOICE commands were given, the kids learnt all the patterns by heart, and all they needed was a "tap" on the microphone and the music.

These young people were also all members of the "Ottawa Junior Kennel Club" led my Mrs. Joy Picozzi. She informed me one day that these juniors had been invited to give their display at the CKC Centennial Show in Toronto. Wow, this was a big time. Now try to imagine getting twenty lively children with their dogs to a motel near Toronto, plus mums and dads as well. We made it. Early morning rehearsal on the motel parking lot. Then they all dispersed to visit various places in Toronto, the tower, museums, etc. I was terrified that some of them would get lost or be late for the big event. Everyone told me to simmer down, stop worrying. The hour came near, still not a full crew, Oh my God. Then they were there, ready to go. Nice and smart in club uniforms, dogs all groomed. In they went in front of hundreds of "Dog people"; these were not just average public spectators.

They were wonderful, all the drills, the utility exercises, everything. At the finish the crowd gave a wonderful appreciation to the kids. Not only that, the President of the CKC came to congratulate them as well as sitting in a group photo with them; thank you Dick Meen.

Again I realize how lucky I have been over the years with dogs. Now and again I meet some of the junior drill team, not children anymore, kids have a habit of growing up. Now some are married, some at University, all talk about the drill team and remember the fun we all had.

It was hard work, but the results were well worth it. In the memory mood, I have met and been honored to know some of the finest people in the dog sports world. My belief is that the world is divided into two parts, those who love dogs and those who do not. Thankfully, most of the people I have met have been dog people.

A. Newman

Some absolutely stand out in my memory; from England years ago, my teacher, trainer and friend, Wilf CHADWICK. Other important names that mean a lot to me are Bing Bellamy, trainer and top quality judge; Len Pierce, Kennel Club Working dogs chairman, a leader in progress.

Here in Canada so many good people, Laverne Jackson, judge and very fine gentleman to all he met. Martha Covington Thorne, a real lady in all ways; excellent dog handler and a person who understood every dog she handled. Well known for her absolute top dog in the show ring "Hornblower", so many Best in Shows with Martha. She was so kind and helpful to those of us who were not so smart in the ways of the show ring. My big day came when my big male Rottweiler "Kaiser of Mallam", to my surprise, we were awarded best of breed, this meant going on to the "group" class. When I saw that Martha and "Hornblower" were also in the group I thought to myself, that's got to win, he was so beautiful. Off we went, trotting around the ring, judge looking all serious. Then the shock, "Kaiser" took the best in group. I could not believe it. Next thing I knew was Martha giving me a huge hug and lifting me off the ground. She explained you have done it, the first Rottweiler handled by owner to win the group. I asked her, what about Hornblower? She replied, has got plenty before, and he will do well in the future so don't worry about him; enjoy your dog and your day.

Now you know why I will never forget this lady, to me she was the "First Lady" of the Canadian confirmation ring.

While I am on the goings in the show ring as opposed to the trials ring, I remember a little problem that I had at a show. Within each group of dogs, they are exhibited in alphabetical order, so with my Rottweiler leaving the ring after being judged, the Samoyed dogs were next in. It is always a rush to get into and out of the rings, especially if the hall is crowded. Most people are very good and keep their dogs close and under control. However, as Kaiser and I were leaving the ring on the first day of the three day event, we struck a problem. A Samoyed, on the end of a long leash dived and nipped my dog. I asked the "haughty lady owner" to please control her dog. She replied, Oh don't bother me, nice eh.

Next day, same procedur3e, but I was ready, I got between Kaiser and the big white brute. It still dived and hit my knee. I did snap at the lady and told her that if it happened again the next day I would let the leash go and Kaiser would meet his unsociable opponent on fair ground.

An angry Rottweiler is not to be ignored.

Sure enough, the next day as I came out of the ring, I dropped my leash. When the sweet lady saw this she dived back out of the way very quickly. I just told "Kaiser" to leave and we walked by with no trouble. This little incident however did stay in my dogs mind; he did not forget the Samoyed "Nip".

This let to problems if we won the breed class. I had to run my dog in front of the winner of the Samoyeds. Kaiser was upset at this dog behind him. I did learn to avoid the distraction, as we galloped round the ring I did, accidently, of course, loose my hat. I stopped to pick it up, and then joined the runners "behind" the Samoyed. Kaiser felt better when his enemy was in front of him, in fact he did move a lot better with lots of drive. Another learning day for me.

Beware of some bad mannered and ignorant exhibitors.

There are always ways to avoid problems with out making bigger ones. To his last days Kai never did like big white dogs. I don't think I am a spiteful person, but some little incidents can get my back up. I do not forget them. I think that I see some of these incidents as a challenge.

At a show I was introduced to a lady who had just acquired a newly recognized breed of dog. It was the Petite Basset Griffon Vondeen. It was a nice looking smaller dog, it had a working background. Suddenly, a man certainly not a gentleman, cut in to the group of us and stated no use going to obedience school, he informed the new owner, I am going to have the first PBGV ever in Canada to win an obedience title. This pissed me off, if you will please excuse the crude expression. I said to the lady, if you come to my place two mornings a week for about an hour work, I will help you all I can to cut that snob down to size, no charge. She agreed and we worked hard for about five months, and then entered the dog for novice tests. The lady and the dog did so well; three trials and they had the first CD title in Canada on a PBGV.

After the prize awards, I asked if I could borrow the dog, I found the man, showed him the ribbons and advised him to control his attitude towards others who obviously could do what he could only mouth off about.

I went home happy.

I often feel the same way when people say, "my stupid dog will not retrieve, or he is too stupid to track his own dinner. Do not let these people realize that the shoe is on the other foot. They are too stupid to teach the dog to achieve these abilities. Show the dog, help the dog and the dog will amaze you. Just think of all the tasks that dogs do for us humans: Guide dogs for the blind, Police Service dogs, drugs and explosive dogs; digs that are used to detect and trace arson at fires; military mine detector dogs; the dogs who rescue people from all situations, drowning, avalanches, earthquakes and more.

What it all boils down to is the "Status Quo" or "what we have now is the best possible". In fact there are some elements who consider the current obedience tests much too difficult for the average dog.

When you consider the abilities of the dog outside the obedience ring, does it not make you think? The small dog i.e. under 10" in height has no problem jumping up on to the owners lap while sitting on a chair, which is at least 20" high. Why then is the test jump height set at 4"?

Our working friends with the retrievers and gun dogs expect the dog to jump at least 30" with a bird or rabbit in its mouth on a retrieve. No one considers that to be excessive and cruel, just natural. Of course it is the responsibility of the owner to make sure the dog is well conditioned and physically fit. Maybe that is why we see so many dogs in trials failing the hurdle, bar jump and broad jump. Poor conditioning, not physical impossibility.

The constant lowering of the standards for average dogs does seem to be the recent trend of regulating bodies in the working sports. This trend now seems to be spreading to the "Stay" exercises. Consideration is being seriously given to shorten the sit and down stay times. Please do not do it. The system of "honoring" in tests is the obvious answer to the boring line up for sits and downs. One dog works all the tests required while another dog is in the ring on a down stay. Does this not prove two things, one the "down" dog is obedient and capable of keeping the position, and it also proves that it will not move during the distractions of the dog working the tests. It also eliminates the line ups and waste of time getting dogs in and out of the ring to do nothing but keep still with no distractions. Hey, life is full of distractions.

Getting back to the dogs ability to learn if the humans have the ability to teach.

A local group of owners of "Setters", English, Irish and Gordon's approached me to show them what the agility sport was all about. I agreed, and fourteen dogs and owners met in our training hall early one Sunday morning.

Slowly and gently the dogs were introduced to the equipment. With care and encouragement the dogs were physically guided over and through the various obstacles. The jumps nice and low to start were no problem to any dog. The tunnel was kept very short and all the dogs began to enjoy going through, they joined in the fun. The "A" frame kept at waist level was not problem after the first few climbs. Then the dog walk, 12 foot ramp on and off, with the center 12 foot level at waist height. By guiding the dog with one hand in the collar, the other reached over the rear end to keep it against the human's hip, the dog could not fall. Gradually they found their feet, all four of them, and walked the plank. The sea-saw, set very low at 12 inches, the dogs were stood on the plank and gently rocked to get them used to the motion, then walked up. At lunch time the sport was explained to the owners, points and time faults, etc. At the end of the day, all the dogs and handlers could navigate all the lowered obstacles, except one dog who did not, could not, would not deal with the sea-saw; can't win them all. In one full day, the dogs learnt to learn and the owners learnt to teach.

The main reason for the dog's success was the total attitude of the humans who understood their dog and encouraged and helped the dogs to overcome something new and build up the dog's confidence. The only equipment that is not natural is the weave poles. These require careful and consistent practice. Dogs climb, dogs jump, dogs go down holes. Show them, they will do it our way. In return for the Setter agility day, I was invited by the Club to attend a full day field and water training promoted by the Ontario group.

I must be honest; I never really had a feeling for retriever trials, I like to watch them work, but not for me to train. The only input I had was to be a "gun" at a few trials in England. Over the years I grew out of the shooting interest. I had seen too many guns in my life.

I found myself out in the bush beside a nice still lake. The instructors first checked all the dogs for fitness; they fired the odd shot to see if the dogs were not "gun shy". Then the water work. Dummy birds were tossed into the lake, the dogs were helped by owners to go out and retrieve in shallow water, then the deeper stuff with weeds and bulrushes. Most of the dogs were naturals, real water babies. Next lesson was to trail or track birds in the bush. Dead birds were dragged through the grass and bush, then the dogs shown how to use their noses to find them.

Lunch was a very "elegant" affair full course, pheasant of course and a little wine and coffee; very nice. Finally a display of the trained experienced dogs; retrieving from water, jumping with birds over 30 inch jumps delivering to hand. A great display. I just did not think my Rottweiler, Border Collies or German Shepherds would be so gentle with the birds; they would probably either spit out the feathers or try to eat them. Another wonderful dog day out and learning more about dogs.

I still hear ignorant, but well meaning people say that Setters are a few bricks short of a full load, plus other disparaging remarks. All I can say is go watch the Setters work at the sport they were designed to work at.

All dogs are different by breed, size, shape and temperament within each breed they are each an individual and it takes a smart human to discover this and to adjust the training and handling to the individual dog. That is the mark of a good dog man or woman.

Oh my god not a Siberian Husky, I have heard it, you have heard it. Comments like, "they are bred to pull" and nothing else. Or, do not take that leash off or he will run at least ten miles before you catch him".

I admit in my early days of fooling about with dogs, if a Sibe appeared, the hairs on the back of my neck went up. That was in my "stupid" days, now I know much better than goodness. This revelation occurred solely because of a group of owners of the Sibes came to me for basic obedience. It did not take long for me to realize that these people knew their dogs. It was so obvious by the way they handled them and even by the way they spoke to them. It became a challenge for me, I really wanted to help these people to gain good success with their dogs; Sibes are thinking dogs. They are dogs with an independent nature. They also can do everything we ask of them if we go the right way about showing and helping them to WANT TO DO IT. That is the skill and understanding that the Sibe owner must acquire. During the period of a week, we have about a dozen Sibes working basic obedience or agility. It was a bit of a struggle at the beginning, but due to the efforts of the owners things settled down very well. There was so much potential in these dogs and it all began to develop into good work.

Remember many of our Sibes are in teams of sled dogs. They did well in the races and of course loved the freedom of the trails and the snow. To also be able to be worked in the current "automatic" obedience exercises as well to a good standard, good enough to enter CKC obedience trials and qualify for their titles. I am sure that this year many more will do that.

The hard work that the owners are putting in with obedience is certainly paying off with the agility dogs. They are amazing, this year half of the K9 Cup teams that we enter are made up of Sibes. Next year, I hope we will have a full team of Sibes. We now have the three teams in the K-9 Cup; The Artfull Doggers, the Artfull Puppies and the Artfull Graduates. What name shall we have for our Sibe team; any suggestions?

To watch these dogs on the field is rewarding, they go over and under all obstacles, fast. Sometimes they get the wind up their tail and do a few extra circuits, but who cares, it is the fun and enjoyment that counts, not the ribbons, but we do get a pile of them anyway. To see the Sibes, Shepherds and Shelties all together on the field or in the training hall gives me a good feeling, add them to the Cockapoo, the Spaniels, miniature Aussie and MinPins, what a wonderful variety, all getting on well with each other.

The owners, what can I say about these people, all working together, all helping each other. They are the first people there when the jobs are to be done, painting equipment, moving it so the grass can be cut, all the jobs that have to be done to keep the club running. It is a privilege to know such people.

QUESTIONS

Q.   Is there such an animal as a dog that can not be trained? This is a question that I am often asked. How do I answer this?

Basically I say "No", any dog can be taught to do "something". The answer lies in the activity that you wish to teach.

There are people like me who never became brain surgeons, top lawyers or artists, why?

It is not their inclination or ability, but the same people did rise to be respected in their chosen profession or way of life, even politicians, whoops, sorry about that one.

If you only teach a dog to fetch your slippers, or bark to be let out, that is training. I like to see the pet dogs do a "rollover" or play dead. That may be the extent of it's ability. Not every dog is a future obedience Champion, an agility Master performer, just as humans have limits, so do dogs. The smart thing is to recognize these limits and stop forcing the dog to achieve something that he is not capable of. The human "ego" plays a huge part in this gross mistake.

Q.   Are some of the equipment used in training dogs cruel?

Good question, a short answer, with limitations and qualifications "NO"

Lets look at the "Training collar", better known and unfortunately used as a "Choke Chain"; a length of light chain with a ring at each end; simple, the universal tool for dog training.

Minor problems: Too short or too long

Put on the dog the wrong way

The better name would be "Snatch Chain" it should be used as a "JOLT" not pulled so as to prevent the dog breathing. Again dogs are smart, they can brace the muscles in the neck and still keep pulling. If they chain is fractionally loose then snatched, the dog can not brace, he gets an effective correction at the right split second he needs it. It is a handler skill to sue the training collar correctly and effectively. Put yourself in the dog's neck and just think what you are doing to choke a dog, yes it is cruel.

Q.   Would you ever use a "Pinch or Spike collar"?

Answer is yes, there is a place in the right "experienced" hands for a pinch collar.

What is a Pinch Collar?

A chain made up of BLUNT links that when jerked tight pinch the dogs neck all around.

With a hard unfeeling tough dog the pinch is an excellent tool. Used properly as a behavior deterrent he can not ignore it, notice I say used properly. Used at a 90 degree angle from the neck, the links will pinch only. If pulled off center it will tilt and cannot pinch but dig into the neck if pulling sideways.

The pinch collar is for experienced trainers and handlers. In the hands of an inexperienced person it can cause pain, even damage. The owner who makes his dog wear a pinch collar 24 hours a day just demonstrates his ignorance of training, and just uses the collar as a crutch or physical constraint.

Q.   Would you ever use the "Ear Pinch" when teaching a dog to retrieve"?

Short answer is yes, as a very last resort and only if it is so necessary and vitally important to the owner.

What is the "Ear Pinch"?

It is a system of holding the dog's ear flap between the thumb and forefinger, squeezing hard until the dog yelps and opens his mouth to allow you to put the dumb-bell in, then releases quickly and praise the dog.

As I have said, a last resort if the owner thinks it necessary. It is very effective if done properly, to a dog of good temperament. A system NOT to be played with; in over 50 years I have used it twice on police service dogs.

Does that tell you something?

Q.   How do you feel about the use of food to train a dog?

In general I like to teach by praise and correction, with praise I include giving the dog a toy or ball when any exercise is completed with success. I do like to give a tiny piece of kibble, cheese or liver when a dog comes on recall and sits close and straight in front of me. In many cases I have watched dogs being given food much too often. In one case I counted the food reward in heel work that lasted approximately fifteen minutes, the dog received twenty eight food rewards. After each movement, i.e. heel, halt, turn, slow, fast and on and on the dog was bribed and fat!!!!

I feel myself that if my praise and petting after success is not enough, then there is something wrong with me. On the recall that little extra special makes the dog happy to sit in front of me. I need that for recalls, retrieves and scent returns.

Q.   How do you feel abut the "Clicker" training?

The clicker training is a neutral sound, anyone can use a clicker. It is not a voice communication between my dog and I.

In class I observed, when one student use the clicker, all the rest of the class dogs looked for the usual food treat that follows the sound.

Clickers are not a new idea, at one time brass chains with ornaments that rattled were used to make a mechanical sound.

My dogs learn my voice and verbal sounds, by which they know if I am pleased or not so pleased with them. A nice clean tone lets them know all is well. A low growl or grunt, call it what you will, lets them know instantly that whatever they are doing does not please me. Voice, praise and love, not clickers and bribery to extreme.

THE FUTURE

Why do I keep working with dogs?

I am well past my "three score and ten" years, nearly up to the four score mark, so why not sell up and go and live in a seniors residence? Eat cucumber sandwiches and drink tea.

Simple, I could not survive it. I keep my life with dogs as a pleasure to me, not other answer. The joys of helping people who arrive with problem dogs, and after they work so hard, the dogs become so different; the satisfaction that I feel when the dogs progress and become real obedient and the happy family members.

Over the past thirty five years of the "All Dogs Sports Club" many dogs have gone to very high standards in competition, if that is what the owner's enjoy. Before I stopped counting titles at trials a few years ago, we had over fifty past students gain the Obedience Champions title, many, many through to the Open titles. We lost count years ago of the Companion Dog Titles. Quite a few went on to get tracking dog titles under the CKC and AKC, some Bermuda as well.

During our SchH period many dogs achieved SchH I and SchH II, three went on to the SchH III.

Now a days Agility is the main sport, our students have led the way for others to follow.

Titles and top competition are fun for those who partake in them. There are some really wonderful and satisfying achievements of which I am so pleased to have a small part in, nothing to do with shows and trials: the deaf lady with a deaf dog that overcame their problems to be able to work in competition; the handlers in wheel chairs who also worked so hard to train very successfully for trials and life; the tough dog who came first night wanting to attack anything that moved, man or beast, to see this dog a few months later working off leash with other dogs in the class.

On the other side of the coin, the shy frightened dog that was afraid of his own shadow. After months of the owners love, patience and care, becoming a happy and relaxed dog.

These are my rewards after all the frustration, problem solving and quite a few prayers.

When I was younger and a lot swifter than I am now, I enjoyed all the different dog sports. From scent handling, retrieve the ball hurdling to search and rescue tests. As I got older I began to realize that ribbons and trophies and titles are for the human ego, the dog has no idea why they are being pushed, sometimes a little too hard to perform. I saw too many "Gaps" between owner and dog, the success in the ring was the be all to the human. Bonding did not seem to count.

I know we all love our dogs, but sometimes we forget to stop and think, am I pushing my dog too hard, is he or she really capable of the high standard and effort that I want and demand? We should all stop and think about this now and again.

Over the years I have seen some very mechanical and unfeeling training of dogs. The key being "do it or else", I hate to think what the "else" is when dog and owner are alone.

We all delight in our dogs being sociable and friendly with all the other dogs they dome into contact with.

What about the owners and their sociability with each other. Is it a case of get in the class, work the dog; go home with no interaction with the other people. This does happen, why not get to know your fellow students, let them help you, and you help them. It makes for a wonderful class atmosphere. Just as going after class together to MacDonald's or Tim Horton's for a coffee and a chat together, usually a few laughs as well.

So I am old fashioned, I feel that all my students dogs are my dogs as well, all the students are my friends, not just instructor and students. Many of these friendships have lasted a life time. So not only are the dogs a pleasure for me, the friends I meet also gives me a reason to keep going.

I hope some of the experiences I have mentioned in this scribble are of interest. Some may not agree, that's fine, we all have our ways and opinions.

That is all about my fun and disasters over the many years. For interest, the last section is a compilation of the various tests and exercises that dogs all over the world are capable of performing and do each week.

If I had one regret; it is the continual lowering of standards for the tests in North America. My last line should upset a few.

The dogs in Europe can do it, why can't the North American dogs do it as well, or even better.

"Oh What a Tangled Web We Weave"

Note: not complete, there are more!

AAC National Agility Trial, 2002
- Entries -

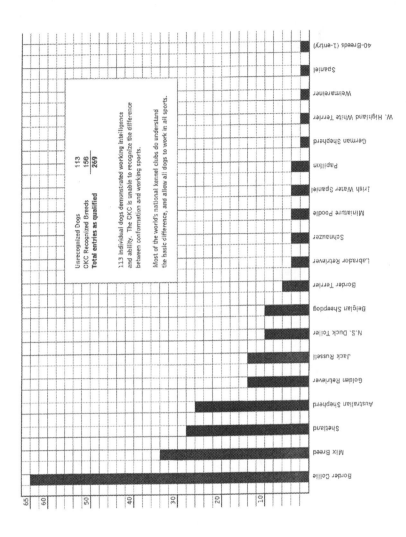

Unrecognized Dogs   113
CKC Recognized Breeds   156
Total entries as qualified   269

113 individual dogs demonstrated working intelligence
and ability. The CKC is unable to recognize the difference
between conformation and working sports.

Most of the world's national kennel clubs do understand
the basic difference, and allow all dogs to work in all sports.

Entries by Class Change Over
or "To Those Who Have Will be Given"

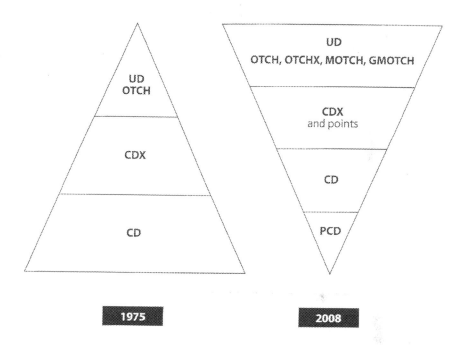

Five titles for utility dog test. No progress for novice, the roots of the sport.
This is the situation of the balance of the sport of obedience today, due to
the CKC board's lack of foresight and effective promotion, and control,
also the acceptance of poor advice from obedience councils.

Rule 6.1.16
No badges or clothing with club identification thereon, shall be worn or displayed by exhibitors / handlers when exhibiting in the ring.

Rule 8.13.9
Dogs shall not be picked
up and carried in any
Obedience ring. The
penalty shall be
substantial.
(not applicable to
Conformation ring)

Rule, regulation, or old wives tale?
No judge and exhibitor who are officiating or exhibiting at the same
show or trial, will travel in the same vehicle to the show or trial.

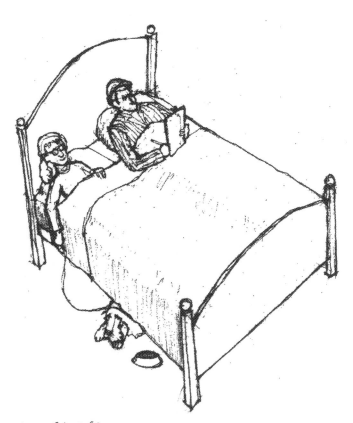

True or fairy tale?
No judge and exhibitor will stay in the same accommodation if both are judging
or exhibiting at the same trial.

CHAPTER THREE

FROM PRESENT DAY TO THE FUTURE

In my previous scribbling I have tried to show a wonderful life with dogs and people, both in Europe, North America and even Africa.

I have been so lucky to meet so many people who have encouraged and helped me over the past fifty years in so many different and varied dog sports. It is now that I am much older in the tooth I can sit back and appreciate the good life that I have been blessed with. I can only hope that this came across in the earlier pages.

The fact is also that, over the years the "regulating" Bodies have not managed to progress as much as the owners, trainers and instructors of the dogs. What you are about to read, I hope, is being discussed where ever dog people get together; shows, clubs and even pubs.

The problem is that the hopes, dreams and comments never seem to be discussed and considered at all the various boards and counsels that meet to "promote" dog sports. Not that I expect the majority of dog people to agree or accept my opinions, ideas, or if you like, my "whining".

I just hope that it may be a seed for discussion maybe a possibility for some improvements in our sports.

A. Newman

The Canadian Kennel Club (CKC) is the National Dog Club of Canada. The CKC has assembled and for most part, made public a new "Strategic Plan Analysis", 2009-2011. This plan has been divided into four main headings:

Strengths / Weaknesses / Opportunities / Threats

There seems to be a feeling of power in the basic fact that the "Federal Government of Canada has "appointed" the CKC as the Ministry of Agricultures Agent to carry out the registration, etc. of most of the pure bred dogs in Canada. Oh yes, there are other agents for other purebred dogs in Canada, i.e. Border collie registry. As a registry, the CKC does carry out the regulations t have been laid down by the Federal Government and is compensated for this duty, or service. The "<u>STRENGTH</u>" comes from compliance with the "Animal Pedigree Act"; the benefit is the financial arrangement.

Next the "<u>Broad range of programming</u>": Yes, this is a fact. The CKC does indeed offer many dog activities and sports. There is, and it cannot be denied that of all the activities, the main and first priority is the promotion of conformation. It would be difficult to state what percentage of the CKC is devoted to the other activities such as those described as, the performance elements of the dog events. Breed standards, breed judges and promotion of "New breeds and Rare breeds" have accounted for the majority of board deliberations and efforts.

A "<u>Large and energetic membership</u>": In the past few years the energy seems to have dissipated. Entries are down at events, numbers of general members at AGM is smaller. It is doubtful if new members each year are more than the members who do not renew memberships. The totals do go up and down, but in general considering the possible total available, it is not encouraging.

The "<u>Publisher of "Main" canine material in Canada</u>": Quite a statement when compared with other National Kennel Clubs across the world. Rule books, yes. Magazine, the CKC owned and now published by the CKC on its own. Why waste time here, it is a total disaster today. Enough said, maybe some comment later.

Board, Committee, Council expertise: Most boards are formed from members who are experienced in breeding, conformation; there are now even professional handlers on the recent boards. Could there be discrimination, bias or even lack of experience of the other sports activities? Has any board member withdrawn from a discussion or vote due to conflict of interest, (or income). The next main heading that the planner has identified is "Weakness".

A weakness is considered to be the Diverse interests of members: If the CKC promotes a "Broad range of interests", how can it be a weakness? Surely it must be the inability to proceed to promote the interest that is a problem. One lady told me, it is simple, "the CKC have bitten off more than the administration can chew".

Now we see "a weakness in the growth of membership": We were told earlier on in the analysis that we had a large energetic membership. Which is it? Of course we could always do with more members, but how does the CKC intend to get them and keep them:

It was suggested in the past that to enter a CKC event, everyone should have to be a member. I remember that one; it went down like a lead balloon.

Next weakness, a "Perceived lack of response time from CKC office and staff": This is not just "perceived" it is a general complaint of members. In the past year, I sent three letters to the office; I have NOT received either a reply or acknowledgement. If I phone and leave a message, no one calls back this is a matter for the CEO to deal with. It is a simple management problem.

We always seem to have limited funds to use for the promotion of the objects and policy of the CKC. Why? In the current world financial situation was it advisable to at the right time to set up a charity foundation, are we in the position to dish out cash to very well deserving projects? As usual, up go all the fees and memberships. What's new?

Low public profile: Grow up; the NON dog owning public does not know that the CKC even exists.

The third heading is just as interesting as <u>opportunity</u>.

<u>International linkages</u>: For international, please read America Kennel Club, period.

The only international interest that the CKC has is the pedigree and registration of a few countries to enable breeders to import and export dogs. We love the AKC Westminster Show; brave hearts even fly to the KC Crufts show. When it comes to international working sports we have problems. We do not, and it seems will not adjust to comply with the rest of the world sports standards. At the so called International Obedience trial in Europe, the tests and exercises were adjusted and lowered to permit North American dogs to compete.

We have to "BEND" our rules to attend International Agility Trials in Europe, CKC even allowed our wonderful Border Collies to represent Canada overseas but they are forbidden to enter in Canadian trials.

Recently in the official pages of the "Dogs in Canada", we saw a motion offered and passed that the CKC would no longer recognize any judge of the Fédération Cynologique Internationale (FCI). We were in formed that the CKC was playing "Tit for Tat" as the FCI required judges, all judges to judge to the international standards. As Canadian judges are required to judge to the CKC standards, they are not complying with the FCI rules at FCI shows. Can we not get it all together? Reminds me of a bunch of kids playing street hockey, one says it my puck, if I cannot play in goal; I am going home with my puck.

Could not negotiation and concessions be agreed, give a little, take a little.

Thank goodness the CKC does not have guns or we would be going to war with the FCI (are we?)

At the very bottom of the heading for "opportunities" we find, <u>Fund Raising</u>: We have already moaned about limited funds.

What are the two main ways to improve a financial situation? First promote, increase income. Second look inward, save and cut waste. One does not have to look far to find "small" waste items. Little minor items will all add up to saving dollars, and as a side product increase efficiency of CKC operations.

Personally the first economy that comes to mind is from the finance department. I receive four (4) envelopes a year, each contains another envelope and a financial statement that tells me I am in credit, (financially at least) with the CKC. The four envelopes, the paper invoice and four (stamps). Plus computer time.

I know I am in credit. Just remind me ONCE a year please. Anyway, why the extra envelope, I do not have to send anything back. Magnify these mailings and figure out how much it costs. A question I asked before but did not receive an answer.

If all entry forms from all the shows and trials plus other events have to be sent by club secretaries to the CKC from all over Canada. What happens to this pile of paper? Where is it stored? How much space does it take up? For how long does it sit there? Commercial floor space is valued at approximately $100 to $150 per square foot or more. How much does it cost to store all these forms per year?

Hey what an idea, why not require club secretaries to KEEP the forms safe for the year. If the CKC needs a form to check, just send the one they ask for. No storage space very little mail costs. Is this not saving a few dollars?

One of my club members have a joint membership with his wife, a nice reduction of fee. They only read ONE copy of the Dogs In Canada, the official pages and only one copy of the Dogs Annual. He has asked the CKC to only send them <u>one</u> copy. They have a joint membership so do not need or even want the two copies. You guessed it, no answer; the two copies of everything still come through the mail as usual. Is this not an opportunity to save? Is this not administration or house keeping?

The last heading of the Strategic Plan is "<u>THREATS TO THE CKC</u>": The Anti-Dog Legislation comes top of the list. Of course the CKC objects to the vicious and uncalled for legislation; very poorly thought out by some politicians, written by public servants and lawyers who have not the slightest knowledge about the subject. It is a mess.

The CKC does give verbal support to the small groups who are actively fighting the law, but does the CKC offer any financial help? It seems that only registered charity groups are helped – no charity registration, then no financial help from the foundation.

My favorite of all the threats that the CKC perceives "OPPOSITION from EXTERNAL INTEREST Groups":

This is interesting because it does not make it very clear as to who these groups are. Some of the violent militant animal protections must be included. What about the investigative media programs, the anti-dog breeders brigade who tell half truths and only publish the bad side of any situation. Well do not get worried, newspapers die the day after, television programs and brief news clips soon follow? It is their duty and the object to find the truth and deal with it.

The expression "softening" of some entries at shows and trials is a "gentle" approach to a large and serious problem if the sport is going to survive in its current set up.

What causes the radical loss of entries? Is it the expense of entries, cost of travel, hotels and food? Those seem to be discussed at the ring side.

High cost of entries: What is involved in promoting a dog show trial?

CKC license fee

Cost of venue

Judges transportation

Judges accommodation

CKC Fee from entry

CKC Fee miscellaneous dogs, etc.

Prizes, etc.

Labour to set up, etc.

Agents fee for registration service

Catalogue cost

Average Entry fee in Canada is $28.00

Average Entry fee in Europe is $5.00

Average cost of Judge in Canada is $400 total day

Average cost of Judge in Europe is $100 total day

Selection of Venue – Canada is STATUS

Selection of Venue – Europe is SUITABLE

Weather: It snows in Canada

It rains in Europe

Those expenses are high; can they be reduced in any way? Mainly Judges fees controlled, selection of "suitable" venues opposed to "status" locations with long gowns and nice tuxedoes and flowers.

Many great shows and trials are held in "Fields, drill halls, and parking lots".   ????

Many Judges who love sport consider it an honor to be asked to judge, some do consider an appointment to be an occupation or a form of regular income.

These first few pages are mainly observations of the report of the Strategic Plan 2009 – 2011.

Any owner, exhibitor or breeder is going to be affected by the CKC board's attitude and action of the plan.

The full plan is available on the PC system at the CKC.

What will happen between 2009 and 2011? If history and initiative of the CKC is considered: very little.

However onwards and upwards, or in most members' opinion: upwards and downwards.

You must be thinking that I am so biased against the CKC, I am not. As a life member, showing dogs to breed Champions, and working CKC in all classes with at least ten dogs over the past fifty years it has been both fun and rewarding.

I have been able to attend many annual general meetings all over the country, Toronto, Calgary, Montreal, and Ottawa. In fact for a brief, very brief time I served on a versatility committee, then realized that whatever the members suggest was never going to get very far either in the administration or the board table.

If there is anything that I will never understand about the administration and governing of the sport of dogs, is the total and absolute divisions between the conformation sport and the many varied "working sports" or as the CKC describe them, the performance events. The word performance as in a bunch of canine circus tricks to be performed by dogs that do not make the standards of the show ring because of size, shape and color. It does exist, it is there. It is like an unholy marriage that no one wants to get into.

One answer would be a divorce, or at least a clear separation. The conformation could concentrate on show, breeding, registrations and transfers, plus import and export of dogs.

The working elements could just train and compete in their favorite events without the influence of the breeder and show exhibitor fancy emanating from the boards decisions, or lack of them.

The division of the CKC into two very separate departments, a small working dog council to refer matters, with experience to the full board for processing; this can be done. Remember the only interest that the Federal government has is the sanctity and accuracy of breed recording. The Minister has no interest OR mandate over non-registerable dogs; or any of the working events.

The recent referendum vote to exclude all non registerable dogs from working events was **not** an overwhelming victory for the breeder members of the CKC. With 65% vote where as the other referendums were passed by over 90%.

Remember, few working dog owners will join the CKC, it has nothing to offer them, and there are no benefits. So with the majority of votes cast by NON WORKING members the outcome was to be expected.

Just what did they reject? Thousands of more dogs entered into the CKC system with all the entry fees and the growth of obedient, well trained dogs across the whole nation. Many "pet" owners enjoying a great recreation and sport.

On condition, that a few of my breeder friends suggest, yes I have some, to spay and neuter every non registered dog who wishes to enter a working event would that help control the stray population, and give a little security to the breeders who fear they might lose puppy sales.

The survey company contracted and paid $x, seem to have provided a plan. There are a few glitches in it, but it is now in the CKC's power to take some action. Minor tinkering will not solve the problems.

All we can do is wait and see.

TO PROMOTE WORKING SPORTS

Many people with much more experience and knowledge that I shall ever have, should step forward to suggest and make improvement required to make conformation a more enjoyable sport.

My concern is the administration of all the working dog sports. The current situation has many flaws. We are still working our dogs to a system and standard that was basically designed in 1947. A mish mash of exercises and tests that was suitable then. No one wants to turn the sport of working dogs upside down with outrageous radical changes. If we just remove our North American rose colored glasses and look outside the domestic scene to discover what progress has been made in the rest of the world.

Handlers and owners want to be able to take their dogs overseas to international events but to do this, all of the world must play to the same rules. We have domestic sports events titled "World Championships" the obvious sport is baseball. Are Canada and the USA the world? Where are the Cuban and the Japanese teams in the so call "World" competition? At least the world soccer event is open to all nations; they all play the sport to the same rules.

It can happen if we have the will to make it happen.

North America has sent teams to Europe to compete, for many years, the sport of Schutzhund has sent National teams from both Canada and the USA, and they have both done very well. The reason is that all the SchH clubs train and work to the "International" rules, not a made in North America set of rules and standards. Also the sport is not regulated by the CKC or the AKC, basically the FCI. All other nations have tests and exercises with the same names as ours, but there the similarity stops.

The minor amount of heel work in the CKC tests does not cover the extreme testing that is normal in European heelwork. Suffice it to say the average time in the CKC and AKC heelwork test is less than 60 seconds. In Europe's heel work you must demonstrate heeling for an average of 4 minutes. It will include all turns, including left about turns as well, and will be carried out at all three speeds, the dog is put into the three positions; sit, stand and down as the handler is moving, then returns to pick up the dog still on the move.

It is so interesting, both in the training hall and in the trial ring. It is also a huge challenge to attain this quality and standard of "Obedience". With a few minor additions and small changes in the tests for novice and open obedience routines, the progress and higher standards would be obvious.

A few little changes, for example, why not include a retrieve any article in the novice class, why not introduce a send away into the open class. Both these additions would both spice up the test and at the same time prepare the dogs for the next higher class.

So you see, there is no need to "Wreck" the system to improve the standards and quality of work. Where the most improvement and innovation is urgently required is in the North American Utility Dog test, or after it!!

As it is now it is the highest test in the trial schedule, the problem is that after the UD test what next?

The answer is nothing. Just go on and on repeating the same routine over and over for ever. Of course you can pick up another three magnificent titles if you keep doing the same tests and getting high scores for points. Would it not be the benefit of the sport, the trainers and the dogs to introduce a new test of a very high standard into the system after UD?

An ex CKC board member told me my "dream" was unnecessary, look at the high entries in the UD class. Of course the entries are high, they have nowhere else to go, nothing else to train and work for. I do agree with his principle, "if it ain't broke, don't fix it". What about the low entries in the novice classes today.

That is "broke", so why not fix it? Remember all Obedience Champions stared in the beginner or novice class. Gradually there will be fewer at the top level if we do not do something about the lack of beginners, starters or novice dogs and handlers today. The worst we can do is to sit back and wait for it to happen. Then we will say "How did that happen"? Do something NOW.

Still on the subject of obedience tests and exercises that have the same description, but not the same way of working, how about the name of an exercise in the Utility Dog class. We call the test, "Scent Discrimination", when we all know it is in fact a scent "Identification", and it is the handler's scent that the dog is required to find and retrieve. It is a strange dog that does not know its owners scent. Basically the dog is trained to ignore ANY scented article except the owners. That is NOT discrimination. Event if some stewards do touch some of the articles, it is only the owners scent that attracts the dog.

We should rename this test to "Owners Scent Identification Test". Wow, that should upset quite a few of the utility class handlers!!!

Then what is "Discrimination"? It is the ability of the dog to be given a scent <u>other</u> than the handlers and to seek and find another article with the same strangers scent from a group of articles or cloths with have also been scented properly, i.e. handled well by two stewards.

How is this test set up?

First we require ten articles to e on the floor for the dog to work.

Seven are "CLEAN", i.e. laundry fresh untouched by anyone.

Two articles are well handled by two stewards, and then placed out on the Judges instructions.

At this stage we now have nine articles or clothes laid out.

The Judge has "TWO" articles that he or she well handles. When the Judge is ready, one cloth or article is given to the handler; the other is placed out with the other nine.

The handler gives the Judge's scented article to the dog. There are many ways permitted, to fold it over the dog's nose, to drop it in front and let him take the scent.

When the handler is ready, he removes the scented cloth, and sends the dog to "Retrieve" the target, the Judge's cloth from the group of ten. With a good retrieve and present and finish the test is over.

The dog has discriminated between two stewards scent and the Judge's scent that the dog was given.

Main point to note is that there usually is a different Judge, and possibly different stewards at each trial. Just training the dog to retrieve only the handler's scent would not get you very far in Europe.

The system might sound involved, but it is not. We do this in our club just as a fun exercise. If European dogs can do it, so can our wonderful Canadian Dog's. A fully copy of the test is attached for those interested to look at it. Maybe try it!!!!

TEST "C"

SCENT DISCRIMINATION

Scent Discrimination. Judge's scent on a piece of marked cloth. Neutral and decoy cloths to be provided by the Show Executive. The judge shall not place his cloth in the ring himself, but it shall be placed by a steward. A separate similar piece to be used for each dog and the total number of separate similar pieces of cloth from which the dog shall discriminate shall not exceed ten. If a dog fetches or fouls a wrong article this must be replaced by a fresh article. At open-air shows all scent cloths must be adequately weighted to prevent them being blown about. The method of taking scent shall be at the handler's discretion but shall not require the judge to place his hand on or lean towards the dog. A separate similar piece of cloth approximately 6 inches by 6 inches but not more than 10 inches by 10 inches shall be available to be used for giving each dog the scent. Judges should use a scent decoy or decoys.

NOTE: Scent Discrimination – A steward will place the scented article amongst up to a maximum of nine other articles.

In a scent test if a dog brings in a wrong article or physically fouls any article (i.e. mouths it) this article will be replaced.

The dog should at this time be facing away from the articles. On command the handler should bring the dog to a point indicated, give the dog scent and stand upright before sending the dog to find and retrieve the appropriate article. The dog should fin the article and complete the test as for the Retrieve test. In all tests, scent articles are to be placed at least 2 feet apart. Limiting the time allowed for this test is at the Judge's discretion.

Another test exercise that you might like to try is the send away. A simple test, all you need is a marked spot or area about four feet. You can put chalk lines on or tape to mark it.

All you do is set your dog up straight facing the target, and then send him by command. The dog should go straight out and when in or near the area, the handler gives a firm <u>DOWN</u> command.

All of the dog must be INSIDE the target for full marks. This send away is followed by a "recall" as the handler is being directed to walk by the judge, when ordered by the judge to "Call", the handler gives the command; the dog leaves the target and quickly comes to the heel position with the handler.

A nice exercise, a lot of fun, but demonstrates accuracy and response to commands, three in fact. Go out, down, and heel. I hope the little sketches of other tests around the world will interest those handlers that have an adventurous nature. I doubt if many of the UD repeating people will appreciate new exercises and tests.

While mentioning some maybe radical changes for experienced dogs and handlers, I would like to offer another very contentious idea to encourage or attract new people to the trial ring.

What if the inconsequential new CKC test and title of PCD's, Pre Companion Dog was withdrawn and forgotten as a disaster. Could it be replaced by another quite normal and effective test? We all know the companion dog test so well; it is the basic routine that is taught in every self respecting dog training club. Many beginner handlers find the current routine of the CD test a little terrifying, due to the strict no encouragement permitted to the dog, or the penalty for the odd tight leash or extra command. Could we not have a definite class for real beginners within the trial system?

A class exactly the same as the novice (CD), but with some help to the dog and handler by permitting encouragement.

This should <u>NOT</u> be a class for titles, but a class to earn credits, prizes or awards. This could be entry level for new handlers; of course any handler that has ever received a qualifying score in any title class would not be allowed to enter. This is to get new handlers into the sport in a not so formal and strict attitude.

A pass or fail would be fine, I am sure that the majority of the judges could cope with it; in fact many would enjoy helping new handlers into the sport.

Compared with the PCD tests, it would at least make sense.

I am beginning to think that with these radical suggestions and weird new ideas, will it be safe for me to even go to an obedience trial again? Much less go to a CKC Annual General Meeting even as an observer. Do you think that they will take my life membership away on the grounds of treason or treachery?

Honestly folks, this is not hate literature, just comments and opinions that sit in my head after sixty plus years of working dogs. Maybe I should have stayed out on the moors as a shepherd with my faithful Border Collies. Ah well. There are people who think so.

Another element of dog working has almost been destroyed in Canada.

I refer to the sport and joy of tracking with a dog. This pass time must be one of the most rewarding to both handlers and dogs.

To go out as a pair to an open space, find where another human has walked a while before and follow the exact trail, even finding any items and articles that the layer of the track has lost or dropped.

The thrill of watching a dog nose down following each and every step. Remember you cannot do this, even if you got down on your hand and knees, your nose would still be useless.

To see the turns and corners and the indication of the dog finding an article, then going on to the end of the track is so exciting and you realize that this is the dog's natural ability in nature.

The unpleasant fact is that official tracking trials are now few and far between. Clubs just cannot afford the huge cost of promoting a trial.

Main problem is the limitation of number of dogs that judges are allowed to judge in a day. If the CKC limits are so restrictive the cost of each entry is exorbitant. The cost of the judge's fee, the transportation and accommodation when split between eight or ten dogs is just crazy.

How can judges in Europe manage twenty five dogs a day, I did many years ago. Canadian judges have to be so restricted and limited. Setting out tracks the day before and having the judge there for an extra day does not make sense. Neither does laying the track TWICE in twenty four hours. Is this not double laying? The CKC tracking rule book in 1986 contained eight (8) pages. By 2001 it contained twenty-eight (28). The board had not finished then.

In 2007 we held it down to thirty-two (32) pages, only!!

In the official pages of the Dogs In Canada there was a small note that the tracking tests and rules were being "reconsidered". Maybe someone realized that adding more tracking titles, as the "Urban tracking Dog and the Urban Tracking Dog Excellent" was not the route to take to encourage beginners into the sport. It certainly did please the few, very few advanced handlers and their dogs.

Again, as in obedience, the CKC promotes the top end of the sport and virtually ignores all the problems of getting new people.

Where does the advice come from to legislate backwards? I do not think there has been over powering tracking experience of the members around the past few kennel boards of directors.

Wonder what they are considering? So do I.

As in obedience, the tracking standards are not high.

If I could find a tracking trial that I could afford to enter, what would I expect my dog to achieve for his test.

Tracking test rules, January 2007, CKC:

10.7.   The track shall not be less than 400 meters (1312 feet) and not more than 450 meters (1476 feet)

    The track is to be no less than on half hour old, or more than two hours.

The scent shall be of the track layer, who shall leave a leather glove or wallet, satisfactory to the judge, at the end of the track.

All turns shall be well out in the open where there are no fences or boundaries "to guide the dog".

There will be a maximum of five (5) turns, two (2) of which will be at right angles (90°).

No turns will be of acute angles.

No conflicting, or cross tracks will be laid.

These requirements are perfect for the beginner tracking dog. Who if successful is awarded the TD title? Of course pages from one to twenty have all the admin information, so it is vital to read and learn them as well. Get a rule book.
Copies can be obtained from the Canadian Kennel Club for a fee.

The Tracking Dog (TD) is attainable by most dogs, of all breeds, some better than others.

Problems arise when looking to improve the quality and the quantity of the actual track. We do not increase the length of the track to say 1,000 <u>yards</u>. We do not add more turns, no real acute angles.

We do not increase the number of articles.

We do not increase the age of the track.

We invent new titles.

Overseas it is normal to extend all these points far more than in North America.

To be awarded a Tracking Dog (TD) titles the dog must also carry out the basic tests:

Heel Free

Send away and directional control

Group 1	Speak (Bark) on Command
	Down stay 10 minutes
	Steadiness to gun shot.
Group 2	Scale 6 feet (can be adopted as "A" frame)
	Clear Jump
	Long Jump
Group 3	Search for articles
	Track and find minimum 3 articles.

If the dog passes in all three groups the title of TD is awarded.

When you see a pedigree form the Kennel Club (UK) now you know the difference between most European and North American titles, and appreciate the work of those handlers and dogs to achieve those standards.

One of the most amusing elements of our obedience system, and it is creeping into the Agility Sport as well, is the standards for the jump heights.

The CKC Jump heights for obedience are very simple.

Vertical jumps bar and hurdle.

The jump is the height of the dog at the withers.

Broad jumps are double the height at the withers.

So the jumps are set to suit each individual dog's height.

There are NO jumps in KC (UK) obedience routines.

For Working trials the dogs are divided into three groups:

	Vertical Jump	Broad Jump	Scale Board Jump
Under 10"	18"	4ft	3ft
Under 15"	24"	6ft	4ft
Over 15"	36"	9ft	6ft

They all do it every weekend, hundreds of them.

Copies of CKC Agility Rules & Regulations can be obtained for a small fee from

The Canadian Kennel Club
200 Ronson Drive, Suite 400
Etobicoke, ON, M9W 5Z9

If you are a member of the CKC you can download them from the web site: www.ckc.ca

Rules for the Agility Association of Canada from:

www.aac.ca

For "Working Trials" from:

Kennel Club (UK)
1-5 Clarges St.
Piccadilly, London, UK, W1J 8AB

Why do these addresses appear here?

It is amazing the number of people who train and enter trials, have never read the rule book of their sport. Now they can compare the standards of the world. If you play the sport, get the rules and in a small way support the organization that supports you.

With these few notes I hope it has demonstrated the whole differences of standards across the world.

Why? We all have the same dogs why can we not all work them to the same international standards?

It is a case of the people, not the dogs.

For the sake of a few dollars, or a few minutes on the www, we could find some interesting facts about our sports around the world.

COMMUNICATIONS OF THE CKC

When this subject is brought up around the clubs and at ringside, the predominant statement that is heard is: What communications?

Official documentation regarding registrations, transfers and imports & export usually dealt with reasonably, that is if the applicant has been so careful to dot the i's and cross the t's. If all the paper work is correct, then the system does work quite well.

As the Federal Agent for those matters it should work well. Problems arise when most other matters are referred or requested of the CKC. Eventually most are dealt with if you are very patient, even pushy!! First and foremost, people should understand that Admin matters are not the responsibility directly of the Chair and members elected to the board. These problems are the direct responsibility of the senior member of the staff employed to operate the administration of the office and the staff employees. What are the most prevalent matters that the membership comments upon? First excessive delays in the system. We all thought with the computer set up, everything would go smooth and quickly. The phone system that gives better access to departments would help. We forgot that computers have to be set up to carry out tasks, it is necessary to leave phone messages when the person you need is not available. It is the same for all operations and business. What is not acceptable is when messages and requests are recorded and never answered. It happens; even when a request is made and received by a staff persona, it is not expected that the request can be answered on the spot at the time. It would be nice to receive a return call with the information requested or even a letter of explanation.

These are the comments of many members. I say again this is the responsibility of the Senior Staff member, the CEO. Directors have far too much work at the board table, they must or should be "hands off" the daily running of the administrative staff. A liaison with the chairman is essential, and co-operation is vital and the INTERNAL communications should flow effectively between them.

The communication of the board's intentions as well as their decisions should be in the pages of the "Official Section" of the Dogs In Canada magazine. Is it? Why separate the magazine, are there secrets in the official pages?

Regarding intentions and decisions; do we ever get any warning regarding the motions that the board is going to discuss? Are the membership ever invited to submit and suggest any ideas BEFORE the decisions are made; which brings us to the system that, only after at least six months delay, do we find out what decisions have been made. The Official pages are published every month. Information could be and should be made public regarding any matters that affect OUR SPORT before the board makes final decision. The exception is in the case of an emergency.

The "Dogs In Canada" magazine does not carry CKC information although it is owned and produced by the CKC. Where are the pages that are of interest to members? The story of a service dog is interesting, as is the history of long gone breeds, at least as they originally were. A page on showing and preparing to show a dog; articles on obedience training, maybe introduction notes to the agility sport, how to get started. Technical articles about illness and disease are not generally readable.

What IF:

A dog food company sponsored a training page, maybe two or three companies, and not just huge colored adverts. People would read these articles. The CKC controls the D.I.C., why not communicate

CKC matters that do affect the readers both members and attract potential members.

The steady decline of the D.I.C. is obvious; the CKC recognizes 127 breeds for conformation. Why has the massive majority of breed clubs stopped offering their breed notes? Each month only a dozen clubs are listed today; apathy, lack of interest? Promote the breed clubs, promote the sports; let's get back to the days when we looked forward to the magazine and read it, cover to cover. We appreciate that "Dogs In Canada" does support itself, even brings in a profit. Is that the sole object of the publication today?

Talking of communication, it does seem that the Discipline committee is the hardest working group of people in the councils and committees. Pages of their deliberations are published each month.

Do the other councils etc ever hold meetings and make suggestions to the board? Will their ever be a public article of the subjects that they discuss. Somewhere, sometime, they must hold meetings or even telephone conferences. Would it not be possible for any interested member to obtain copies of these council deliberations? Many years ago, I used to receive a copy of the obedience council minutes. We discussed these with our club members and were happy to be "In the loop", we even sent our feelings and suggestions to the Chairman, who incidentally sat down with me at the off hours time at several annual general meetings that chairman was of the opinion that meetings were not secret. Of course, the next appointed chairperson told me that I was not entitled to be privy to their discussions. AH WELL, different folks, different strokes.

All I can hope for is that the club will think that all the discussions, reasoning, then their decisions do affect all the interested members. Remove the secrecy, promote more openness and the result will be more interest and understanding of the boards decisions, where their advice came from and the effectiveness of the councils and committees.

Getting back to the first point raised by the "Strategic Plan" Analysis 2009-2011 communications and perceived lack of response; these two matters alone would bring us all closer together.

Once again, all the comments may seem so anti CKC. All of these have been mentioned by so many people around the rings, in the training halls and some have been brought to the attention of directors, board members in the past and even the present. If these pages just make people think, not even agree, it will have served its purpose. I do not expect to see changes in my life time, but I do hope that all dog owners can say that they have a good life with their dogs as friends.

Well that is it. The end of my diatribe; I hope that not too many people are upset, that was not the object. The advance and progress of the working dog sports is the hope, prayer and plea.

Thank you to Denise for all the many hours of translating my handwriting into beautiful type manuscript; Dana for the wonderful graphics you designed for me; Dominique for converting my twisted sense of humor into the funny cartoons and keeping the meaning so clear.

I admire anyone who has the fortitude and courage to read this from cover to cover, how the hell did you do it?

So finally

Last Kick At The Can!

A. Newman

REPORT OF THE CANINE DEMOCRATIC COUNCIL (CDC):

Held over six months ago as seems to be normal; new rules, edict and advice to be complied with.

1. Each canine that enters a show or trial ring will have a tag attached to its ear. The tag will be yellow and will contain the canine number and its breed. This will prevent Border Collies from intruding into either sport.

2. Each canine will be lifted, weighed and measured by the judge, unless the judge is suffering from a hernia.

3. Male canines will be checked by positioning a mirror under the rear legs to ensure that the male is intact. No judge will touch the canine. The principle is, "To do as you would wish to be done to you".

4. All canines of a white dominant color will be lifted and well shaken by two stewards to remove all the chalk powder or other coloring substances.

5. All canines with a black nose will be checked with a damp cloth to detect mascara or other black stuff. The same procedure should be followed on canines with black spots in strange places.

6. All canine movements around the ring will be in waltz time, Clubs will provide the music.

   German Shepherds only will march around the ring to the sound of military band music.

7. No handler of any canine may speak to the judge while the canine is being shown or tested. Messages may be relayed by a steward or by cell phone.

8. Only Canine Democratic Council approved bait, kibble or treats may be given in the ring, unless they are provided by the dog food company that is sponsoring the show or trial.

9. A quiet area, away from the general public, must be set aside for exhibitors that have not been awarded points or qualifying scores. The comments and language of such will not be recorded and children will not be allowed in the area.

10. On entering and leaving the rings, each competitor will bow to the judge and remove headdress. The licking of the judge's boots is not required.

11. All canine handlers will wear on their backs, as for sports teams, the name of their breed, this will assist the judge as to what breed is in the ring. There may be problem with this rule regarding the width of the handlers shoulders when showing the Nova Scotia Duck Toller Retriever or the Petite Basset Griffon Vondeen.

12. Every judge should measure the sit position beside the handler. The use of a protractor is advised as any variation of more than five degrees should be considered to be a crocked sit.

13. Any canine that "fouls" the ring or show area will be guilty of an offence against the environment and will be reported to the Federal Minister of "Green" for possible discipline.

14. The wearing of the "Pet Knicks" is advised for all female canines, this is due to disgusting manners of some canine males.

15. Methane gas is toxic, therefore the feeding of Baked Beans before any public show or trial should be carefully considered.

16. In future all miniature, toy and Standard Poodles being exhibited in Quebec will be required to qualify in a "Barking in French Test". Exemptions will be make for those canines that have both parents educated in any English language obedience training schools.

17. It is important that all exhibitors entered in any event to be tested for steroids or other chemicals; this may apply to any handlers that smoke.

18. No foreign show or working titles should be shown on any entry forms, etc, this may attract attention from the Canadian Border Guard Services and may result in being referred to the immigration department for security investigations.

19. Do not refer to any Municipal By-Law Enforcement officer as a "Dog Catcher". If ever your canine is "Dog-napped" you will never get it back.

20. Do not get over excited if you see a canine pulling a cart. It may be just owned by a person that has their car repossessed, or it may be a modern edition of the NDP Barretmobile in these hard times.

21. The anthem "How Much is that Doggy in the Window" will be played at all shows and trials. This will expedite the sale of all the puppies that have been sold by breeders to the pet stores, and help to get them out of those hell holes.

22. Any competitor in tracking trial that manages to get all tangled up the in the tracking line, thus it impedes his progression any part of the track, will be marked as "failed" and may be cut free at once.

At any trial outdoors in pouring rain, any canine that breaks the stay exercise and hides under the stewards table will be marked as "Passes". This as the canine obviously has more intelligence than the handler.

Notes